STUDIES IN
MODERN HEBREW LITERATURE

GENERAL EDITOR
DAVID PATTERSON

ABRAHAM MAPU

ABRAHAM MAPU
From a portrait drawing by A. Grodzensky

ABRAHAM MAPU

THE CREATOR OF THE
MODERN HEBREW NOVEL

By

DAVID PATTERSON, M.A., Ph.D.

Cowley Lecturer in Post-Biblical Hebrew
University of Oxford

MCMLXIV
EAST AND WEST LIBRARY

MADE IN GREAT BRITAIN
PRINTED AND BOUND BY
BUTLER & TANNER LTD, FROME

For

SARAH PATTERSON

CONTENTS

ACKNOWLEDGEMENTS

The author wishes to express his sincere gratitude to the many persons from whom he has obtained encouragement and advice, and particularly to Dr M. Wallenstein and Emeritus Professor H. H. Rowley of the University of Manchester, Professors C. Rabin and S. Halkin of the Hebrew University of Jerusalem, Mr R. May and the directors of the East and West Library, for their sympathetic interest and their many helpful suggestions. Not least, his sincere thanks are due to his wife for her constant encouragement and help at all stages of the work.

PREFACE

THIS study of the novels of Abraham Mapu is the first volume of a series of monographs devoted to a literary appreciation of the major writers in modern Hebrew. The desirability of publishing such a series requires little explanation in view of the almost total dearth of serious studies in this field in English. The novels of Abraham Mapu may be regarded as the first productions of real merit in modern Hebrew literature, and they have exercised a powerful influence on its subsequent development and on the renaissance of Hebrew as a modern language. They are equally important for the impact which they made on the segregated Jewish communities in eastern Europe in the second half of the nineteenth century.

Each monograph in the series will present an outline of the selected author's background, followed by a brief biography and a serious literary appreciation of his work. It will also include a representative selection of his writings in English translation. In this way it is hoped that the interested layman and the student of comparative literature may gain an insight into the quality of modern Hebrew writing and the development of Hebrew literature during the last hundred years. The notes, references and bibliography are designed to increase the value of the series for the serious student. The system of transliteration from Hebrew into English is based upon the one employed in the *Jewish Encyclopaedia*, New York and London, 1901–5. As personal names and titles of books are principally involved, such a simplified system appeared most suitable.

PART ONE

NOTE

The following abbreviated titles appear in the notes:

Mapu.   *Kol Kitebei Abraham Mapu* (*The Collected Writings of Abraham Mapu*), Tel-Aviv, 1950. All references to Mapu's works are drawn from this edition.

Klausner. J. Klausner, *Historiah Shel ha-Sifrut ha-'Ibrit ha-Ḥadashah* (*History of Modern Hebrew Literature*), Vol. III, second revised edition, Jerusalem, 1953.

The references to the Hebrew Bible have been drawn from R. Kittel, *Biblia Hebraica*, 3rd edition.

A PEOPLE IN FERMENT[1]

A CENTURY and a decade have passed since Abraham Mapu published the very first Hebrew novel—incidentally, the first novel in a Biblical setting in any language—and at one stroke created a whole new realm in Hebrew letters. Since its original appearance in 1853 the scope of Hebrew literature has broadened beyond all recognition, and it now encompasses a rich variety of literary form, written in a far more complex and subtle idiom than that employed by Mapu. Technical experience and linguistic resources have so improved in the intervening years, while such elementary literary skills as characterization, plot-construction and the art of dialogue have meanwhile so developed that Mapu's novels necessarily appear somewhat naïve and immature. Nevertheless, the creative artist who dares attempt some new and unfamiliar pattern, or casts his expression in an untried mould, needs imagination, courage and tenacity of high order. Even when he accomplishes the rare feat of winning immediate recognition and acclaim, posterity alone can estimate the real significance and the validity of his experiment.

This study, then, is devoted to a critical examination of the literary qualities of Abraham Mapu's three surviving novels[2]— *The Love of Zion* (*Ahabat Ziyyon*), *The Guilt of Samaria* (*Ashmat Shomeron*) and *The Hypocrite* (*'Ayiṭ Ẓabu'a*).[3] Of a fourth novel, *The Visionaries* (*Ḥozei Ḥezyonot*), a small fragment of seven chapters is alone extant, so that only occasional

---

1. A fuller and more detailed summary of the events outlined in this introduction may be found in such standard works of reference as, e.g., H. Graetz, *History of the Jews*, Vol. V, London, 1892; S. M. Dubnow, *History of the Jews in Russia and Poland*, Vol. II, Philadelphia, 1918; L. Greenberg, *The Jews in Russia*, Vol. I, New Haven, 1944; A. Ruppin, *The Jews in the Modern World*, London, 1934; J. S. Raisin, *The Haskalah Movement in Russia*, Philadelphia, 1913; J. Meisl, *Haskalah*, Berlin, 1919.

2. For details of first publication see below, pp. 22 ff.

3. Throughout this study the titles appear in English translation, the Hebrew originals being given in brackets only here.

reference has been made to that work, which reputedly comprised no less than ten whole parts. The disappearance of the manuscript spelled personal tragedy for its author; it must be regarded as an equally tragic loss for modern Hebrew literature.[4]

Since the first moment of publication all three novels have proved firm favourites with the Hebrew reading public, a fact to which some ten editions of *The Guilt of Samaria* and *The Hypocrite*, and no less than fifteen editions of *The Love of Zion*, bear ample testimony. The latter, indeed, soon became the first 'classic' in modern Hebrew literature, and has been translated into a wide variety of languages, including Russian, French, German, English, Arabic, Judaeo-Arabic, Judaeo-Persian, Ladino and Yiddish.[5] Although *The Love of Zion* nowadays shares the fate common to so many classics in being relegated to the schoolroom and appealing in the main to the younger reader, its influence on the course of Hebrew literature in the second half of the nineteenth century and even in the early part of the twentieth can scarcely be overestimated. A considerable proportion of the major Hebrew writers during the last one hundred years have readily admitted their indebtedness to Mapu's first novel, which for many served as the first introduction to the very concept of literature as such.[6]

Two of the three novels under review, namely *The Love of Zion* and *The Guilt of Samaria*, are historical romances set in the ancient land of Israel in the period of the prophet Isaiah, and spanning the reigns of Kings Ahaz and Hezekiah in the southern kingdom of Judah. The third novel, *The Hypocrite*, is a tale of contemporary Jewish life in eastern Europe, in which the author attempts to outline the conflicts raging within his own society and suggest mild palliatives for some of its more obvious weaknesses. But although the historical romances are

4. See below, p. 23.

5. See below, p. 24, note 61. Of the English versions, the first appeared in 1887 under the title *Prince and Peasant*, but it is an adaptation rather than a translation. The second appeared in New York in 1903, entitled *In the Days of Isayah*. Both versions are virtually unobtainable.

6. See below, p. 27 f.

separated in time from the contemporary novel by no less than two and a half millennia, all three reflect an astonishing similarity of ideal and aspiration. All of them may be regarded as the progeny—in many respects, indeed, the consummation—of an intellectual ferment, to whose tenets Mapu remains, perhaps, the last wholly-committed adherent of real stature in Hebrew literature.

This intellectual ferment, which was destined to play a decisive role in subsequent Jewish history, arose as an expression of revolt against the physical and mental restrictions of the ghetto, first imposed in the middle of the sixteenth century and subsequently maintained for some two hundred and fifty harsh and bitter years. Effective opposition to the humiliations of such legal inferiority may be traced to the small but wealthy Jewish community in Berlin in the second half of the eighteenth century, at whose head stood the illustrious figure of Moses Mendelssohn.[7] Stimulated by the impact of the humanitarian ideals emanating from France, and by a more tolerant attitude in certain influential sections of society, a movement grew up within German Jewry, whose object was the emancipation of the Jews and the amelioration of their material and cultural condition.

Modelled on the German *Aufklärung*, the Hebrew movement of enlightenment, known as *Haskalah*, attempted to provide a bridge in Jewish life from the medieval world of the ghetto to the modern world of western Europe. As the first step, it advocated a reform in Jewish education calculated to facilitate Jewish participation in the broad stream of European culture by grafting secular elements to a syllabus hitherto entirely composed of traditional, religious studies.[8] For the *Maskilim*, as the exponents of enlightenment were called, some understanding of European culture appeared to be an essential prerequisite in the long, hard struggle for emancipation.

Mere changes in the school curriculum, however, were clearly not enough. If the debasing effects of the ghetto were

7. See D. Patterson, 'Moses Men- *Between East and West*, London, 1958.
delssohn's Concept of Tolerance', in   8. See below, p. 98.

to be annulled, measures had to be sought to bolster the self-confidence of the Jewish people, restore its dignity, reawaken its emotional life, quicken its aesthetic sense and generally counteract the stultifying consequences of long isolation and confinement.[9] A serious attempt to solve these very formidable problems became the primary concern of the exponents of *Haskalah*. In view of the limited resources at their disposal, however, the efforts of the *Maskilim* were largely concentrated upon the task of fostering a renewed interest in the Hebrew Bible, which could be made to serve many of their manifold purposes at one fell swoop. A realization of the glory of the national past might help to alleviate the degradation of the present; the pastoral and agricultural background and imagery of scripture might serve to re-establish the contact with nature which had been severed by centuries of ghetto life; the exalted poetry and sublime language of the Bible might similarly awaken dormant aesthetic feelings and encourage an interest in literature for its own sake.[10]

The Hebrew of the Bible, then, was to become the main channel through which the Jewish people might be led towards the glittering vistas of European civilization. But in order to enjoy the fruits of European thought and letters it was first necessary to embark upon the laborious task of composing original works and translating a wide range of studies from various languages into Biblical Hebrew. This clumsy and somewhat artificial exercise largely determined the course of modern Hebrew literature for no less than a century, and is primarily responsible for the strange incompatibility of form and content which characterizes so much of the writing throughout that period. The process gave rise, however, to a number of praiseworthy, and indeed heroic, attempts to overcome the serious linguistic limitations which the pioneers of modern Hebrew literature deliberately imposed upon themselves. Of these, the novels of Abraham Mapu remain the most successful examples.

The *Maskilim*, however, were not content to rely upon Bibli-

9. See below, p. 86.　　　　　10. See below, p. 63.

cal Hebrew as the sole method for the attainment of their ends. In spite of bitter orthodox opposition they enthusiastically advocated the study of foreign cultures and languages, particularly German, in order to provide a growing generation, hungry for secular knowledge, with the instruments necessary for its acquisition. With the repressed avidity of centuries, young Jews hastened to absorb the new learning. In the space of a few short years these eager students attempted to catapult themselves through a process of cultural development, which in western Europe had evolved gradually and painfully over two and a half centuries. Small wonder, then, that the effects upon Jewish life were disastrous! In Germany, the path to secular knowledge soon became a high road to conversion. University education and legal equality were purchased wholesale at the price of Judaism. The new Hebrew, which had in most cases provided the first stepping-stone towards enlightenment, was discarded as soon as the student had acquired sufficient German for his needs. Had it been limited solely to Germany, modern Hebrew literature might have flourished for no more than two or three decades. Fortunately, however, seeds of the new movement were carried over to the much more fertile soil of eastern Europe.

The partitions of Poland at the end of the eighteenth century had resulted in the incorporation of a large, well-populated area of Jewish settlement within the boundaries of the Russian Empire. In consequence, the policy of Russian nationalism fervently pursued by the Czarist administration in the nineteenth century came face to face with the spectacle of a numerous, compact and undeniably alien element living just inside the country's western borders. This alien body clung tenaciously to its own distinctive religion, language, mannerisms, habits of food and dress, and constituted a self-contained, inbred and highly self-conscious society, with a widespread, esoteric system of education, and—from the viewpoint of the regime—of highly doubtful loyalties.

In seeking to neutralize this potentially hostile segment of the population, the government resorted sometimes to a policy of conciliation, but more frequently to one of ruthless oppression. During the long reign of Nicholas I (1825–55), the oppression worsened into a nightmare reign of terror, characterized by ferocious assaults on the economic and religious structure of Jewish life, and the introduction of a system of compulsory military service of twenty-five years' duration, with child recruits mercilessly pressed and kidnapped into premilitary training establishments. Few of these Cantonists, as they were called, were ever reunited with their families.[11] The sorry plight of Russian Jewry was further aggravated by a remarkable natural increase in population throughout the nineteenth century, accompanied by a proportional increase in the difficulties of eking out even the meagrest of livelihoods. Grinding poverty became the all-pervading and most compelling factor in Jewish life. The scope of economic activity was so severely limited that a man with a barrel of herrings was considered a merchant!

The first ten years of the reign of Alexander II (1855–81), however, seemed to herald an era of reform. Juvenile conscription was finally abolished, a number of the more irksome economic restrictions were rescinded, while Jewish students were even allowed entry to the high schools and universities previously barred to them. This latter measure, which was aimed at the cultural integration of the Jewish population in place of the prior unsuccessful attempts at religious conversion, received the enthusiastic support of the growing band of *Maskilim*, the Jewish exponents of enlightenment.

The Hebrew renaissance in Germany, though but short-lived, had not vanished entirely without trace. Wandering scholars from the towns and villages of eastern Europe, after making their way to Berlin or some other great centre of enlightenment in search of the new learning, had later returned

11. A most moving account of such an episode may be found in P. Smolenskin's novel *Ha-Toʻeh be-Darekei ha-Ḥayyim*, Warsaw, 1905 (first published in *Ha-Shaḥar*, 1868– 70), pp. 107 ff. As a child the author witnessed his elder brother, himself a child of ten, being forcibly dragged away to military service, never to be heard of again.

to spread the ideas of *Haskalah* in the lands of their birth. To these *Maskilim* the government's educational proposals seemed a heaven-sent instrument for the reform of Jewish life as well as for the eventual acquisition of political and economic emancipation. Hence they embraced the cause of secular education with unabated zeal, urging Jewish youth to take immediate advantage of the new facilities.[12]

The encouragement of secular education, however, excited the bitter antagonism of two powerful forces within the Jewish community—the orthodox Pietists and the Ḥasidim. Both these factions, long at war with each other, launched a combined attack upon the movement of *Haskalah*, in which they at once discerned an inherent threat to themselves. The exponents of *Haskalah*, for their part, eagerly responded to the challenge, attacking the rigidly restrictive traditional education, which regarded all branches of secular study as anathema. They denounced the narrowness and bigotry of a religious framework, which attempted to isolate the community completely from the rapid developments of the outside world, while devoting the lion's share of its intellectual activity to interminable, hair-splitting arguments on the fine points of ritual theory and practice. Against the Ḥasidim they took up the cudgels even more readily. In its initial period the movement of Ḥasidism had represented a new flowering of spiritual activity. By the middle of the nineteenth century it had partly degenerated into a conglomeration of base superstitions and semi-magical practices, under the stress of weaknesses inherent in the system—notably the unrestrained faith in the wonder-working *Rebbes*—which lent itself to exploitation and abuse, and which presented a blank wall to any attempts at mass enlightenment.[13]

12. For a typical example of the enthusiasm which the reforms of Alexander II engendered amongst the *Maskilim*, see the panegyric to the rulers of Russia in the introduction to *The Visionaries* (Mapu, p. 456). The poem expresses the fervent hope that both the Jewish people and the Hebrew language will benefit from the Czar's enlightened rule. Cf. below, p. 19.

13. See D. Patterson, 'Some Religious Attitudes Reflected in the Hebrew Novels of the Period of

To this three-cornered contest, bitterly waged between the *Maskilim*, the Pietists and the Ḥasidim, a further complication was added, a phenomenon arising from the teachings of *Haskalah*, but distressingly unforeseen. The young people, who had responded readily and in growing numbers to the call of *Haskalah* for enlightenment, secular education and entrance to the universities, went a step further, and embarked upon a process of rapid assimilation to the majority culture. Once again the instrument of the Hebrew language, into which the *Maskilim* had so laboriously translated a copious number of foreign works on art, literature and science,[14] was used as a means of acquiring the secular knowledge necessary for entrance to a university, and promptly abandoned.

This had not been the intention of the *Maskilim* at all. For one of their chief aims had been to revive and fashion Hebrew into a suitable medium for the expression of the richness and beauty of life, whereas instead, they found themselves the unwitting abetters of a ceaseless process of complete estrangement from Judaism. The movement of *Haskalah* in Russia never successfully recovered from the shock, even though a similar fate had overtaken it in Germany some fifty years previously, and might not, therefore, have been entirely unexpected. Even during the last decades of the nineteenth century the *Maskilim* still raised the cry of enlightenment and education, although in ever more feeble measure, until finally the poet J. L. Gordon (1831–95), after a lifetime of struggle for the ideals of *Haskalah*, could only utter the despairing cry: 'For whom do I toil . . .?'[15]

Enlightenment', in the *Bulletin of the John Rylands Library*, Vol. 42, No. 2, March, 1960; and 'The Portrait of Hasidism in the Nineteenth-Century Hebrew Novel', in the *Journal of Semitic Studies*, Vol. V, No. 4, October, 1960, and 'The Portrait of the "Saddik" in the Nineteenth-Century Hebrew Novel', ibid., Vol. VIII, No. 2, Autumn, 1963.

14. Cf. above, p. 6. In this context it is worthy of recall that Elijah, Gaon of Vilna (1720–97), had even previously encouraged his disciples to translate scientific works into Hebrew. See N. Slouschz, *The Renascence of Hebrew Literature*, Philadelphia, 1909, p. 98.

15. *Kol Shirei J. L. Gordon*, Tel-Aviv, 1929, Vol. I, p. 76.

Against this complex background the battle of *Haskalah* was fought, and, before the reaction of disillusionment, with a naïve confidence and an intense conviction of being in the right. In very great measure the *Maskilim* penetrated the unhealthy forces at work in the Jewish community, even though failing to recognize the immensity of the stresses and strains at work, so soon destined to bring about the cataclysmic changes in Jewish life, which they proved powerless to prevent. Nor did they understand, until the damage had been done, the negative side of their own efforts, and their own contribution to the undermining of the communal unity—a breach which has never been repaired!

In the meantime, however, they set about reform with a fervent and missionary ardour, so that similar threads of polemic and tendentious writing—although coloured in accordance with the form of expression—may be discovered in the satires of Joseph Perl and Isaac Erter,[16] in the poetry of Judah Leib Gordon and in the novels of Abraham Mapu. In particular, Mapu's long novel of contemporary life, *The Hypocrite*, served as a pattern for the militant, social novel, which has occupied a dominant place in Hebrew literature for almost a century.[17]

The peculiar merit of Mapu's novels thus lies in the fact that they may be regarded both as the consummation of the first major division in modern Hebrew literature, and equally as one of the important formative factors in its subsequent development. It is with the literary qualities responsible for so unusual a dual role that the following chapters are primarily concerned.

16. See below, pp. 54 and 101. 17. See below, p. 105 f.

LIFE AND WORK

No study of the role of Abraham Mapu in the development of modern Hebrew literature can fail to notice the striking contrast between the imaginative life displayed in his novels and the sheer drabness of the life of grinding and relentless poverty which was his personal fate. The narrow limits of his own physical horizons and the dull monotony of his daily routine serve only to emphasize the romantic fantasy which permeates his stories, and to underline the rich and exciting adventures encountered by so many of his characters almost at every turn. Indeed, there is an element of alchemy in Mapu's talent, that serves to translate the dross of a humdrum and humiliating struggle for existence into a golden dream-world of excitement and romance. Certainly, few novelists could have emerged from a less promising environment.

Abraham ben Jekutiel Mapu was born in Slobodka, a suburb of the important Lithuanian city of Kovno, on the tenth of Tebeth, 1808.[1] The Jewish community, numbering some six hundred families, was miserably poor. The low, wooden houses flanking the unpaved streets each provided shelter for no less than four or five families, while hunger—as the growing child learned only too early—was the normal attending circumstance of life. Only the close ties of affection between the young Abraham and his parents could compensate, in some measure, for the poverty-stricken conditions of the home.

His father, Jekutiel, was considered one of the leading scholars of the town,[2] and earned his living by teaching Hebrew. The teacher, or *Melammed*, ranked among the lowliest occupations in Jewish society—at least, as far as remuneration was concerned—and few were they who would resort to it while

1. R. Brainin, *Abraham Mapu*, Piotrokow, 1900, p. 3. According to J. Klausner the eighth of Shevat, 1807 (misprinted 1907). See *Klausner*, p. 271 and footnote.

2. Cf. Shneur Sachs, *Toledot Abraham Mapu*, supplement to the thirtieth-year edition of *Ha-Zefirah*, Warsaw, 1903, p. 16.

any other avenue of livelihood remained open. Suffice it to say that the word 'teacher' had none of the associations of dignity, or a certain social standing, which it carries at the present time. Lessons were usually given in the teacher's own home, the class-room coinciding with the living-room, and extended, even for the youngest, from dawn to dusk. The teacher was frequently a bitterly frustrated man, and often found a sadistic outlet for his anger in savage punishments meted out indiscriminately to his young charges.[3] For the Jewish child life was all study and no play, and the anxieties, normally associated with adulthood, began to weigh upon him only too early.

Jekutiel, however, seems to have been a kindly, though ailing, man, and in spite of his straitened circumstances, succeeded in giving his son the prevailing Jewish education. Abraham's mother, Dinah, was a shrewd and pious woman, more capable than her gentle husband, and possessed of considerable strength of character which, on occasion, she was not afraid to exert on behalf of her son, when she disapproved of the company he was keeping.[4] The young Abraham, though undernourished and weakly, was endowed with great intellectual ability. At the tender age of seven he joined the ranks of his father's advanced pupils, and at twelve he was considered fit to leave the *Ḥeder* or elementary school, and continue his studies alone in the school of advanced studies known as the *Beit-ha-Midrash*.[5] He had already earned the coveted title of '*Illui*, reserved for child prodigies, and early in life he mastered much of the Talmudic learning of the day. Yet such were the teaching methods of that time, and so completely was the study of grammar neglected, that he was unable to compose two or three sentences in correct Hebrew—an unpromising beginning for a future novelist!

At fifteen he was introduced to the mysteries of Kabbala by

3. A vivid description of such a teacher may be found in S. Levin's autobiographical *Childhood in Exile*, London, 1929, pp. 45 ff. Cf. also *The*

Autobiography of Solomon Maimon, London, 1954, p. 31.

4. *Klausner*, p. 273.

5. R. Brainin, op. cit., p. 9 f.

his father, who was himself engaged in its study. It is related that his imagination became so inflamed by the hidden and mystic doctrines, especially those known as practical Kabbala,[6] that he performed an experiment designed to make himself invisible, carefully following the prescribed incantations and rather gruesome directions.[7] Convinced of success, he was bitterly chagrined at being greeted by a friend, while walking home 'unseen'. Although disappointed at the failure of his experiment, he attributed it to the fact that he had not yet reached the required degree of spiritual purity. However, this appears to have been his sole attempt to perform miracles.

In the year 1825, at the age of seventeen, he married the daughter of a well-to-do inhabitant of Kovno. In accordance with the accepted custom which favoured early marriage, but which afforded the parents complete freedom to arrange a betrothal without prior consultation with the principal parties concerned, he saw his bride for the first time on his wedding day. Their subsequent relationship was cordial, but never deep. Indeed, this first marriage seems to have exerted little influence upon him, especially since the young bridegroom was not at first required to earn a livelihood for his family. The father-in-law was normally expected to provide his daughter and her husband with a number of years of board and residence in his own house—a clause to that effect being usually inserted into the marriage contract. Hence after his marriage, Mapu moved to his father-in-law's house, and continued his studies there. While living in Kovno, he made the acquaintance of a certain Rabbi Eliezer, and under his influence began to frequent Ḥasidic circles, to which movement his interest in Kabbala had provided a certain affinity.[8] Neither his father nor mother was pleased at this development, but whereas his father acquiesced, either through tolerance or mere

6. See G. G. Scholem, *Major Trends in Jewish Mysticism*, Jerusalem, 1941.

7. A. Kaplan, *Ḥayyei Abraham Mapu*, Vienna, 1870, pp. 10–12.

J. Klausner, however, casts serious doubt on this somewhat apocryphal story, *Klausner*, p. 274.

8. R. Brainin, op. cit., p. 20.

weakness,[9] his more determined mother intervened personally, and removed her son from the group by force.[10]

Even after his violent leave-taking from *Hasidism*, Mapu maintained his interest in Kabbala, which occasioned a period of close contact with Elijah Ragoler, Rabbi of his native Slobodka, who was also engaged in its study. Their relationship, however, proved fruitful for another reason. During his visits to his friend's house, Mapu discovered a copy of the *Psalms* with a Latin translation.[11] This chance find was of great importance to Mapu's subsequent development; indeed, he was inclined to regard it as the foundation stone of his secular education. It aroused in him a desire to learn Latin, in which language he later became proficient, although forced to acquire it without the aid of a teacher since the study of Latin was virtually unknown amongst the pious Jews of eastern Europe.[12] It has been suggested that his knowledge of Latin may have helped him considerably towards an understanding of the spirit of ancient times,[13] and a comparison of the translation with the Hebrew original may well have caused him to examine the Bible with more detailed attention.[14] Certainly from this time it is possible to trace a growing interest in languages, resulting in the study of French, German and Russian,[15] in all of which he achieved a fair measure of proficiency, in spite of the primitive methods of linguistic study, which were alone within his reach, and the hostile attitude to the learning of foreign languages prevailing in orthodox circles.

The impoverishment of his father-in-law compelled Mapu to seek employment, and to begin the bitter struggle to maintain himself and his family which was to continue throughout his life. He therefore accepted an invitation to become tutor

9. *Klausner*, p. 275.

10. See A. Kaplan, op. cit., p. 12.

11. R. Brainin, op. cit., p. 22.

12. Mapu introduces Latin phrases into his novel *The Hypocrite*, II, 7, p. 280, and in the same work quotes Horace in Hebrew translation, III, 6, p. 335.

13. *Klausner*, p. 278, n. 51.

14. R. Brainin, op. cit., p. 23.

15. Mapu's biographers disagree as to the order in which he learned these languages. Cf. *Klausner*, p. 276 f.

to the children of an innkeeper in a village near Kovno. The living-conditions which he experienced at the inn were even worse than those he had known in his own community. The smoke-filled room, in which he gave instruction, forced him to conduct the lessons sitting with his charges on the floor, where the atmosphere was slightly less polluted! A Catholic priest, who one day chanced upon him in this sorry posture, could not refrain from mocking the 'Schoolmaster'. Surprised, however, at Mapu's apt reply in Latin, the priest aided him towards a more thorough mastery of the language by lending him books from his own library.[16] Mapu remained in the village not more than six months, but during that time, he may have imbibed that appreciation of country life which is so marked in his novels.[17]

His next appointment was more congenial. In the year 1832 he was invited to become tutor to the children of a wealthy merchant in Georgenburg, a small town not far from Kovno.[18] During the two or three years of his sojourn in Georgenburg, he left his wife and family in Slobodka, sending them the whole of his small salary.[19] The separation from his family, however, was compensated in some measure by his introduction to contemporary Hebrew literature, which turned his thoughts towards the ideas of the movement of enlightenment, or *Haskalah*, then being propagated by its exponents, the *Maskilim*. Consequently, after his return to Kovno, where he again spent two or three years, he began to disseminate the ideas of *Haskalah* among the local youth, and acquired something of a reputation for his efforts. But his years of wandering were by no means over. About the year 1837/8 Mapu moved to Rossieny, this time together with his wife and family, and he remained there as a teacher for six or seven years.

Rossieny, at that time, had become a centre of *Haskalah*,

---

16. R. Brainin, op. cit., p. 26 f.

17. See below, p. 40.

18. Mapu's biographers are vague with regard to the sequence of events in the years 1832–48. The order followed here is that suggested in *Klausner*, p. 280 f., who has carefully reviewed the existing evidence in arriving at his conclusions.

19. R. Brainin, op. cit., p. 35.

and within a short time Mapu occupied an honoured position among the enlightened. The happiness he experienced made him conceive a deep affection for the town, which he once described as 'a city of wise men, who love their people and their holy language'. [20] Among the *Maskilim* he met in Rossieny, his most important relationship was with Shneur Sachs (1816–92), who combined a deep love of the Hebrew language with a profound interest in his nation's past. Although eight years his junior, Sachs influenced Mapu profoundly, and encouraged him—according to Mapu's own testimony[21]—to concentrate on Hebrew and the ancient history of Israel.

The years in Rossieny were clouded only by financial worries, to escape from which Mapu petitioned the government for permission to open a school for girls, but without success. In 1844, however, he was appointed to a teaching post in the Hebrew school in Kovno, and returned there, leaving his wife and family in Rossieny.[22] He was able to send for them the following year, but his wife died not long afterwards in 1846. Instead of improving his material position, he had worsened it. His salary was small, and all his efforts to obtain an additional post remained unrewarded. In 1847, therefore, he accepted the proposal of Judah Opatov to become tutor to his son, and moved to Vilna.[23]

Although Vilna was the greatest centre of *Haskalah* in Lithuania,[24] and Mapu became acquainted with such celebrities as Adam ha-Cohen (1794–1878), Samuel Joseph Fünn (1818–91) and Kalman Schulman (1819–99), he appears, nevertheless, to have found the town no more congenial than the house of his employer. Opatov was a harsh and illiterate man, but possessed of great strength of character and prone to acts of violence. When Mapu informed him in 1848 that he had been appointed a teacher in the government school in

20. See ibid., p. 37.
21. See *Klausner*, p. 281.
22. According to *Klausner*, p. 285.
23. See I. Cohen, *History of the*

Jews in Vilna, Philadelphia, 1913, p. 448 f.
24. See J. S. Raisin, *The Haskalah Movement in Russia*, p. 197 f., and I. Cohen, op. cit., pp. 312 ff.

Kovno, Opatov assaulted him physically and Mapu fled his house.[25] Mapu never forgave the insult, and it may well be that he modelled the ignorant but successful boor, Gaal, who plays a leading part in *The Hypocrite*, on his former employer.[26] In spite of his short stay in Vilna and his lack of affection for the *Maskilim* he met there, Mapu was doubtless influenced by the spirit prevailing amongst them. The Hebrew writers in Vilna were characterized by a tendency to Romanticism and a devotion to the Bible and the Hebrew language. His contact with them inclined Mapu in the same direction and formed a natural continuation of the influence first exerted by Shneur Sachs.[27]

The teaching post at the government school proved permanent, and from the year 1848 Mapu resided in Kovno. After leading the life of a widower for several years he remarried in 1851. His second marriage was far more successful, and during the first ten years of his final sojourn in Kovno his slightly more favourable financial circumstances added to the happiness of his domestic life.[28] This was the fruitful period of Mapu's literary productivity, and his fame as a novelist spread rapidly. One of the greatest moments of happiness in the author's life occurred in 1857 on receiving the personal congratulations of Norov, the Russian Minister of Public Institutions.[29] Mapu was always deeply moved by the recollection of this signal honour, and expressed his gratitude to the Russian minister in a poem inserted in the introduction to his novel *The Visionaries*.[30]

The happy years were not destined to continue. His wife was afflicted with a long illness, which severely drained his limited resources, already overtaxed by the heavy expenditures arising from his publications.[31] His troubles were increased by a

25. R. Brainin, op. cit., p. 44.

26. Ibid., p. 45. A. Kaplan, however, denies it, *Ḥayyei Abraham Mapu*, p. 27. J. Klausner considers that Opatov was the model for the character Nehbi in *Amon Pedagog*, *Klausner*, p. 286.

27. *Klausner*, p. 287.

28. Ibid., p. 307.

29. Ibid., p. 308.

30. *Mapu*, p. 456. Cf. above, p. 9.

31. See *Ha-Maggid*, 1861, Issue 41, p. 272.

growing persecution on the part of the Pietists and the Ḥasidim, who bitterly opposed his advocacy of enlightenment, and influenced the censors to delay or even forbid his publications.[32] Even without their hostile intervention publication was difficult enough, and constituted a constant source of irritation.[33] Moreover, from 1860 onwards his own health began to fail. His right hand was affected with palsy, and he was forced to continue writing with his left. His time, too, was greatly curtailed by the numbers of private lessons he was compelled to give in order to supplement his income. In spite of every obstacle, however, his literary activity continued unabated, as his ailing body strove to keep pace with his fertile and tireless mind.

One pleasant incident served to ease the burden of his later years. In the early part of the year 1861, Mapu received an invitation from his brother, with whom he always maintained an affectionate relationship, to spend a few weeks in St Petersburg. The author was delighted with the splendours of the great city, and particularly enjoyed the opera he heard there, which in his characteristic *Meliẓah*[34] he referred to as 'the song of players in the valley of vision'.[35] He returned to Kovno refreshed in mind and body, the pleasant memories of his visit firmly embedded in his thoughts.

His happiness was short-lived. In 1863 his wife died, and he was left alone. In a letter to A. Kaplan, dated 21st Tebeth, 1864, he expresses his wish to marry a third time, preferably a healthy woman of about forty years of age, and mentions two women who have been suggested as eligible.[36] He dis-

---

32. See *Klausner*, p. 313 f.

33. Ibid., p. 311 f.

34. See below, p. 71.

35. 'Neginat ha-Mesaḥaḳim 'Al Gay Ḥizzayon'. R. Brainin, op. cit., p. 67. The phrase is modelled in part on *Isaiah*, xxii. 1.

36. *Kiryat Sefer*, Jerusalem, 1929–30, p. 577. Mapu expresses a like sentiment in a letter to A. S. Friedberg, dated 10th December, 1863, where he states: '. . . But it is not my intention to marry a young woman, but rather one of forty or a little more, a spinster and healthy, for I suffered much from my sick wife, may her memory be blessed, whose illness consumed all my toil.' See R. Brainin, op. cit., p. 69.

misses them, however, on the ground that one is ailing while the other has children. It is the pathetic revelation of a sick and lonely man, anxious to be assured of some companionship in his remaining years. But in the end he remained a widower, continuing to write to the accompaniment of growing acclamation on the one hand, and increasing poverty and physical pain on the other. In 1866, the disease of his fingers returned in an even more acute form, so that every line he wrote became an agony. But he not only persevered with his writing, but even planned new novels, which were to outweigh his previous works.[37]

Towards the end of the same year he contracted an additional illness, this time gall-stones, and his strength began to fail him. When his brother, in consequence, invited him to Paris in 1867, Mapu joyfully accepted his offer, meanwhile determining to undergo an operation in Koenigsberg *en route*. An ardent admirer of French literature and eager to sample the culture of the French capital, he set out with high hopes at the end of the year. But in Koenigsberg his physical condition deteriorated sharply, and he was unable to proceed. In spite of his weakness, his mind remained clear until the end, allowing him to continue with his work, and at the same time engage in literary discussion with the visitors to his sick-bed.[38] He died on the Day of Atonement, 1867.

The origins of Mapu's creativity may be traced to his early twenties. According to R. Brainin the idea of his novel, *The Love of Zion*, was first born as far back as 1830, and several passages were written as early as 1831.[39] Certainly, the long interval between the conception and final publication in 1853 indicates a slow and gradual development. The novel appears to have passed through three distinct stages.[40] While the form

---

37. Ibid., p. 70 f.   38. Ibid., p. 72.
39. Ibid., p. 30 f. J. Klausner, however, argues that it must have been started several years later, *Klausner*, p. 279. He suggests the approximate

date to have been 1843. Ibid., pp. 282 and 328.

40. Cf. A. Sha'anan, '*Iyyunim be-Sifrut ha-Haskalah*, Merhavia, 1952, p. 150 f.

of the first draft is not certain, it would seem to have been modelled on the allegorical dramas of Moses Ḥayyim Luzzatto.[41] The influence of Shneur Sachs, however, directed Mapu's attention towards the Bible, and he chose the theme of Shulamit from the *Song of Songs*.[42] But in its final form, *The Love of Zion* has retained no trace of Shulamit,[43] and the hero and heroine are called Amnon and Tamar.[44] It has been suggested[45] that the work was complete in manuscript form in 1844, but that Mapu was so nervous of publishing it in case the reception should prove unfavourable that he continued to alter it from time to time. The novel was finally published in Vilna in 1853, some three years after its despatch to the censor![46]

The appearance of *The Love of Zion* was roundly acclaimed,[47] and in the four years that followed its publication no less than twelve hundred copies were sold—no mean achievement considering the small numbers of *Maskilim*, and in view of the almost universal poverty.[48] Although Mapu himself complained bitterly that the story was read far more than it was bought, he felt sufficiently encouraged to embark upon further creations.[49] Taking advantage of the more liberal spirit, which marked the accession to the throne of Alexander II in 1855, Mapu chose a setting of contemporary Jewish life for his second work, *The Hypocrite*. This lengthy novel contains five parts, of which the first was published in Vilna in 1858, the second in 1861 and the third in 1864. A second edition containing all five parts appeared posthumously in Warsaw in 1869. Financial difficulties, and constant frustrations due to the censorship, continually delayed publication, causing the author

41. See below, pp. 98 ff.

42. J. Lepin, *Ḳeset ha-Sofer*, Berlin, 1857, p. 103. Cf., however, *Klausner*, p. 282.

43. Shulamit, however, is the name of one of the main characters in *The Guilt of Samaria*. See *Klausner*, p. 282, n. 83.

44. Ibid., p. 295, on the significance of these names.

45. A. Kaplan, op. cit., p. 16.

46. *Klausner*, p. 288.

47. Cf. the praise of Perez Smolenskin quoted by R. Brainin, op. cit., p. 51 f.

48. *Klausner*, p. 297.

49. Ibid.

much needless irritation and worry. But the reception of each separate publication was no less enthusiastic than that which had greeted the appearance of *The Love of Zion*,[50] although the small number of copies actually bought was once more quite disproportionate to the lavishness of the praise.[51]

Simultaneously Mapu had been engaged on the composition of a third novel, *The Visionaries*, dealing with events in the time of the pseudo-Messiah, Shabbethai Zebi.[52] This work was sent to the censor in 1858, together with the first two parts of *The Hypocrite*.[53] The growing campaign of his enemies, however, brought pressure on the censors to forbid the publication of the work.[54] Whereas the publication of *The Hypocrite* was subject only to irritating delays, *The Visionaries* was never allowed to appear in print in spite of all Mapu's frantic and repeated efforts. Worse still, the manuscript disappeared altogether—and was never recovered.[55] To the end of his days Mapu's grief over his loss was inconsolable.[56] Of this work, reported to have run into ten complete parts,[57] only a fragment of seven chapters remains extant.

Sickened by the persecution, which these controversial novels had engendered on the part of the fanatical Pietists and Ḥasidim, Mapu reverted to the Bible for the background of his fourth and last novel, *The Guilt of Samaria*. His great inventive capacity rarely allowed him to be engaged on a single production at any one time. The first part of *The Guilt of Samaria*, written simultaneously with the third part of *The Hypocrite*, was published in Vilna, in 1865. In the same year Mapu produced a second edition of *The Love of Zion*, an unusual but gratifying event within the life-time of a Hebrew writer of that generation.[58] The second part of *The Guilt of Samaria* appeared a year later (Vilna, 1866), when Mapu's

50. *Klausner*, p. 311.

51. Ibid., p. 312.

52. The most authoritative account of the period is by G. G. Scholem, *Shabbetai Zebi*, Tel-Aviv, 1957.

53. *Klausner*, p. 311.

54. Ibid., p. 312 f.

55. R. Brainin, op. cit., p. 65 f.

56. Ibid., p. 66.

57. Ibid., p. 65. J. Klausner, however, produces strong arguments to the effect that only the first part was actually written. *Klausner*, pp. 313–20.

58. Ibid., p. 327.

health had already deteriorated due to the strain of such copious production.

In addition to his novels Mapu, a born teacher, published several textbooks, designed to improve the clumsy educational methods of his day.[59] Of the two such works, Ḥanok Lana‘ar and Der Hausfranzose, which appeared in Vilna in 1859, the former outlines a new method for teaching the rudiments of Hebrew based on the author's own experience, while the latter constitutes a primary textbook for the study of French. Written in German, but with Hebrew characters, it provides an interesting example of the efforts made by the exponents of Haskalah to widen the cultural interests of the community. In the introduction, written in Hebrew, Mapu poured out all the pent-up bitterness accumulated from the difficulties of publication, the small sales of his novels and the fate of his beloved The Visionaries. He expressly states these factors as his reason for producing simple but helpful textbooks instead of working on further stories. His third production of this type was published in Koenigsberg in 1867, and bears the title Amon Pedagog. In this work he portrays his methods of teaching Hebrew. But even within the framework of a textbook his creative talent emerges in the form of a story, which he unfolds section by section as an illustration of the rules to be explained.[60] This was the last publication before his death.[61]

Throughout his life the author possessed a high opinion of the value of all forms of literature, but rated the imaginative story above any other literary genre.[62] He was the first to conceive the idea of a novel in Hebrew, and courageously set about the task of creating it in the face of all difficulties. An appreciation of the measure of his success and an evaluation of his work will be attempted in the following pages. But

59. See, e.g., A. Ruppin, The Jews in the Modern World, pp. 300 ff.

60. The story has been published separately by J. Klausner with the title Beit-Ḥanan, Jerusalem, 1920.

61. For a list of the various editions of Mapu's works see Klausner, p. 333 f. For information concerning the numerous translations of The Love of Zion into a variety of languages see ibid., p. 297.

62. R. Brainin, op. cit., p. 104.

perhaps the most moving tribute to his achievement is that
engraved in three short Hebrew lines upon his gravestone:[63]

> Generations have passed and generations will come,
> But his writings will not be forgotten;
> And the purity of his art will always remain.

63. Ibid., p. 75.

TALES OF VILLAINY
AND ROMANCE

(For a detailed summary of the plots of *The Love of Zion*, *The Guilt of Samaria* and *The Hypocrite* see Part Two.)

THE task of creating an entirely new *genre* in Hebrew literature presented Mapu with a number of extremely thorny
problems, all requiring immediate and simultaneous solution.
Each of the many individual ingredients comprising a novel
bristled with perplexing and unfamiliar difficulties. Form and
treatment, style and language, characterization and dialogue all
demanded the most careful and exacting consideration—in the
absence of any prior Hebrew novel to serve as guide. In spite
of its comparative brevity, it is scarcely surprising that the
author laboured on the composition of his first, most highly
cherished novel for more than twenty years. Yet, formidable
though the various other difficulties of composition proved to
be, the central problem of weaving a sustained and viable plot
remained, perhaps, the most elusive. Admittedly, some of the
themes might well be modelled on one or other of the varie-
gated patterns of the European novel.[1] On the other hand, not
even in European languages had a novel as yet appeared which
drew upon the Bible for its subject-matter. The plots, moreover, were intended to serve a dual purpose. Not only was the
author anxious to compose a romantic tale of heroism and
adventure, but he was equally determined that his stories
should serve as a means of propagating his own particular
ideals.[2] This uncomfortable fusion of didacticism and romance
accounts, at least in part, for one of the least satisfying aspects
of the stories.

Mapu's novels bear certain points of striking similarity. In
spite of the differences of subject-matter and treatment, all
three employ the same principal elements of motivation—love
and intrigue. The theme in each case depicts a struggle between
the forces of good and evil. The former are represented by

1. Cf. below, pp. 102 ff.   2. Cf. below, pp. 86 ff.

characters who are bound together by personal ties of affection and devotion to an ideal, which in the historical novels consists of a deep love of Zion, and in *The Hypocrite* a passion for enlightenment. The latter are embodied in individuals, who are motivated primarily by the hope of personal gain, and who are prepared to go to any lengths to further their nefarious purposes. The interaction of these two sets of forces gives rise to a chain of complex developments, with the initiative principally on the side of the villains, who remain, until the final dénouement, at least one step ahead of the heroes. The latter, indeed, display throughout an irritating naïveté, and triumph in the end—as triumph they must—far more by good luck than good management. But they leave the impression of winning by a rather fortunate knockout, after having been severely outpointed.

Like Milton's Satan in the early books of *Paradise Lost*, it is the villains who—contrary, perhaps, to the author's intention —often command sympathy, and certainly arouse admiration for their daring and resource. The paragon of virtue may awaken respect, but some admixture of human weakness is required to win the wholehearted support of the reader. And so it comes about that the final solution to each plot is somewhat unsatisfactory. The victory does not ring entirely true. Yet there is no way out of the dilemma, for these novels, from the point of view of plot, belong to the class of fiction known as the romance, and as Edwin Muir has pointed out: 'The romance, the novel of action, as it makes the reader suffer occasionally, and as its chief object is to please, must end happily.'[3]

For the modern reader, then, the plots of Mapu's novels contain only a secondary interest. Lacking in originality,[4] depth and subtlety, they must yield pride of place to the style, the language and the setting of the stories. For his own generation, however, the plots, and particularly the plots of the historical novels, constituted the most attractive and fascinating

3. *The Structure of the Novel*, London, 1949, p. 19. 4. See below, pp. 98 ff.

aspect of his work, both because this literary medium was hitherto unknown in Hebrew literature, and because of the quick excitement of adventure which stood out in dazzling contrast against the colourless fabric of his readers' own lives:

> Scarcely had he finished when a troop of horsemen came riding through the wood towards them brandishing their swords—young Ephraimite warriors in rich attire, and at their head a lovely maid, but fearsome to behold with flashing eyes and glowing cheeks. She sat astride an Egyptian horse, emboldened by the gay trappings on his neck, but made bolder still by virtue of his rider set for battle. Her long hair enfolded her firm neck, and she was clad in a loose garment of chequered gold, whose skirts floated as the wind caught them in her headlong gallop. And as she approached the field of tournament, one of the Ephraimite youths cried out: 'Make way, make way for the pride and glory of Ephraim's warriors.'[5]

For a youth whose physical life was confined to the poverty and squalor of a village in the Pale of Settlement, and whose intellectual activity was harnessed to the machine of dry, talmudic casuistry, Mapu opened up a new, refreshing world. The vivid descriptions of heroism and determined action, the free expression of emotion and above all the colourful scenes of a people living unrestricted in its own land inflamed the imagination of a generation starved of life and happiness. The novels were read in cellars and in attics, furtively and in stealth, and never without a quickening of emotion and the gleam of a new and unexpected hope. Above all, they taught a rising generation that life must be *felt* as well as understood.[6] Indeed, the stimulus provided by the publication of Mapu's novels in arousing imaginative and emotional forces long congealed constitutes one of the most striking aspects of his achievement.

Yet, the very impact exerted by his stories piquantly serves to emphasize a major source of weakness in Mapu's plots.

5. *The Guilt of Samaria*, part I, ch. 13.

6. Cf. below, p. 105.

It is paradoxically strange that a power of imagination sufficiently vivid to conceive the urgent need for tales of exciting adventure and romance in Hebrew literature, and one which succeeds so well in conjuring up a convincing picture of ancient Israel, should revert time and again to the use of almost identical themes, and present a somewhat depressing similarity in the construction of the plots, and particularly in the employment of dramatic device.

Of the three novels, the plot of *The Love of Zion* is, perhaps, the most successful by virtue of its comparative simplicity and unpretentiousness, although even here there is a tendency to run wild in the final stages.[7] The brevity of the novel, however, exercises a salutary effect in limiting the complications of the plot, a factor further enhanced by the completely dominating theme of the love of Amnon and Tamar. Both of noble family, the hero and heroine are betrothed from the very womb! By a series of misfortunes, however, Amnon grows up as a shepherd, unaware of his heritage, while his rightful place is taken by the loathsome Azrikam, who also usurps his claim to Tamar. Azrikam's machinations are supported by the villainous Zimri, and several equally unscrupulous accomplices. By saving Tamar's life, Amnon wins her love, and the story pivots upon the wicked plots of the villains to alienate her devotion. So effective are their efforts that all seems lost, until a series of fortuitous coincidences unite the happy pair and restore Amnon to his rightful place. A sub-plot consists in the love of Teman, Tamar's brother, for Peninah, Amnon's sister, which is likewise dogged by misfortune until the inevitable happy ending. The plot is bolstered by mistaken identity, ominous dreams, attempted poisoning, arson, murder and similar melodramatic devices. The romanticism is colourful and unashamed—and for the reader of more sophisticated tastes, absurdly naïve.

The pattern of events in *The Guilt of Samaria* is basically very similar. Although the main emphasis in this novel is on the historical background rather than the individual,[8] nevertheless

7. See chs. 18 and 24.   8. See *Klausner*, p. 340. Cf. below, pp. 48 ff.

several love themes of central importance are simultaneously developed, accompanied by the inevitable series of disappointments and frustrations. The web of intrigue is frequently so bewildering and the much greater length of the novel allows complications to be introduced to such an extent that on several occasions Mapu is constrained to make use of rather tedious repetition to help his readers through the labyrinths of the plot.[9]

The confusion is heightened further by the disguise which two of the central characters assume over large sections of the novel. Uzziel lets himself be known by the significant pseudonym 'Eliada' (God knows), until by chapter fourteen of the second part of the story the two names are used indiscriminately; while Daniel, by a strange turn of events, during which he assumes the name Ammihud, has to impersonate himself![10] The perplexity of the reader may be readily understood. Admittedly the element of surprise and mystery is of great importance, but as E. M. Forster has remarked: 'Every action or word in a plot ought to count; it ought to be economical and spare; even when complicated it should be organic and free from dead matter. It may be difficult or easy, it may and should contain mysteries, but it ought not to mislead.' [11] Only too often the complications of Mapu's novels are both artificial and misleading. In *The Hypocrite*, for example, both Naaman and Eden are reported 'dead' so frequently that the reader is in a constant state of irritating confusion.

The faults inherent in the plot-construction of *The Guilt of Samaria* are, indeed, even more conspicuous in *The Hypocrite*. Here the plot is far too thin for the exceeding length of the novel. At the end of the second part the author addresses the reader directly with the promise of even better things to come! The remark is significant because the story could easily have been wound up at this point, and has to be re-developed to extend over three additional, lengthy parts. The machina-

9. See part I, ch. 11; part II, chs. 6, 12 and 15.

10. Part I, ch. 15.

11. *Aspects of the Novel*, London, 1927, p. 119.

tions and intrigues required to sustain the plot border on the fantastic, as a web of intrigue is spun to entangle the interwoven love themes which comprise the story.

The type of villainies emanating from the arch-hypocrite, Zadok, may be illustrated by the following example, in which four plots are outlined simultaneously in a single paragraph. Hamul is to accuse Nehemiah of using ritually unclean wine at Passover; Obadiah is to denounce Jerahmeel secretly as a spy; Johanan is to steal Elisheba's jewellery until she marries Zarah, and Saul is to be incited against Jeroham, by branding the latter as a member of a band of thieves and by planting some of the stolen jewellery in his home as evidence![12] An even clearer illustration of the ingredients of the plot may be derived from a brief summary of the events of a single chapter:

The wicked Zaphnath is portrayed informing her lover, Levi, that she has just received a letter from her husband, Jerahmeel, expressing his joy at the thought of returning to her. She then unfolds her plan to obtain a divorce. In return, Levi tells her how the real Zadok brought him from Palestine, but died of cholera on the way. He, Levi, thereupon appropriated his letters of recommendation, and later encountered a young man named Hophni who persuaded Levi to let him assume the name Zadok, so that they might claim the inheritance of the deceased. Subsequently he had received a letter from Jerahmeel stating that Hophni had already betrayed two wives. Meanwhile Hophni, established as Zadok, and plotting to destroy Jerahmeel with the aid of Zaphnath, has sent Levi to her for that purpose. Although Zaphnath is surprised to hear that Zadok, Gaal's son-in-law, is really Hophni, she quickly realizes how he may be blackmailed, at the same time planning revenge on Gaal and Nahshon. Levi informs her further that Naaman, although reported dead, is actually still alive, and relates how Gaal had intercepted his letters, which Zadok had then copied in order to demonstrate to Obadiah that his granddaughter Elisheba had been conducting a love-affair with Naaman, and thereby induce the puritanical old man to

12. Part II, ch. 4. Cf. below, p. 50 f.

promise her to his own son, Zarah. He discloses, too, that Gaal is in love with Zibiah, the second wife of Elisheba's father, Eden, the news of whose death has recently arrived. Eden, however, in his dislike for Gaal, had always opposed the idea of marrying his daughter to Gaal's son. Meanwhile Gaal has won the confidence of Levira and her betrothed Julius and is inciting them against Jeroham, Naaman's grandfather, at the same time urging Julius to wean Zimon away from Ruhamah, Naaman's sister. Levi also reveals the fact that Gaal had previously sent an anonymous letter to Zimon slandering Ruhamah, and that Zimon, aroused against Naaman, had stolen the latter's documents and planted letters in his room, making him appear a spy. In consequence Naaman had been arrested and had disappeared, Zimon, meanwhile, spreading a rumour of his death by drowning. Zimon has now become Gaal's clerk and is wooing Ruhamah in order to obtain letters from Jeroham which constitute evidence against Gaal. Levi concludes his disclosures with the information that Zadok is now trying to get rid of him![13]

This single chapter provides a striking demonstration of Mapu's dramatic technique, and contains a large proportion of the weapons in his armoury—complicated love themes, intrigue, revenge, forgery, interception of letters, concealed identity, convenient deaths and defamation of character. It also reveals a marked tendency on Mapu's part to develop his plots via the medium of conversation, so that it appears, at times, as if the action were unfolding in indirect speech.[14] In *The Hypocrite* especially the conversation heavily outweighs the action, which contains neither sufficient variety nor conviction to sustain it. As a result, the many feeble passages inevitably undermine the interest.

This unfortunate tendency is further enhanced by a series of anticlimaxes. When Obadiah, for example, discovers the true villainy of Gaal for the first time, he is so powerfully affected that he faints. The chapter ends on a note of high tension, only

13. Part I, ch. 10.   14. Cf. *The Guilt of Samaria*, part
                                    II, ch. 15.

to be followed by petty and inconsequential conversation, which utterly ruins the effect.[15] This serious deficiency in critical awareness is not confined to *The Hypocrite*. The exciting events in the closing chapters of *The Guilt of Samaria*, culminating in the doom that threatens Zimri's palace, are interrupted with dramatic suddenness. But the reported account of the subsequent action is both lame and disappointing. Mapu's insistence on the heroic part played by all his various heroes, each of whom relates his own particular deeds of daring, is blatantly artificial.[16]

An even more conspicuous demerit stems from the author's overfondness for melodrama. The violence of the first chapter of *The Love of Zion* is re-echoed in *The Guilt of Samaria* in Uzziel's account of the events of his youth.[17] In *The Hypocrite* the atmosphere of 'cloak and dagger' pervades large sections of the story, but breaks all bounds in the description of Shiphrah's rescue from the wedding canopy with the aid of the British consul from Damascus![18] Equally incredible is the scene, reminiscent of Jonah, in which the storm threatening to destroy the London-bound ship is attributed to the crimes of Emil and Zaphnath. They are conveniently washed overboard![19] But even in melodrama Mapu displays a striking lack of variety. The theme of 'house burning' occurs no less than four times in *The Love of Zion*[20] and reappears in *The Guilt of Samaria*.[21] Eliphelet's lion-killing episode in the latter novel[22] is reminiscent of a similar feat performed by Amnon in the former.[23] Tamar's rescue in the latter instance again is paralleled by Adah's rescue from a poisonous snake,[24] while in *The Hypocrite* Shiphrah is similarly saved from drowning.[25] It would almost appear that Mapu considered some comparable rescue as a necessary preliminary for courtship!

15. Part I, chs. 14 and 15.

16. Part II, ch. 19.

17. *The Guilt of Samaria*, part I, ch. 2.

18. Part IV, ch. 8.

19. Part IV, ch. 17.

20. Chs. 2, 11, 21 and 24.

21. Part II, ch. 19.

22. *The Guilt of Samaria*, part II, ch. 7.

23. *The Love of Zion*, ch. 4.

24. *The Guilt of Samaria*, part I, ch. 5.

25. *The Hypocrite*, part II, ch. 9.

The outstanding example of repeated melodrama appears in *The Guilt of Samaria*. In the early part of the story Hephzibah is dramatically rescued by Uzziel from a black Ethiopian, intent on torturing her to death by thirst.[26] Many years later Hephzibah experiences a similar attack by the Ethiopian's son, and is rescued this time by Uzziel's son Eliphelet![27] The coincidence severely strains the reader's credulity, but in each case the description is both vivid and powerful. The episode reveals the best and the worst of Mapu's dramatic qualities. Further coincidences, hardly less incredible, are a common feature. When Amnon, the hero of *The Love of Zion*, is taken captive, the overseer turns out to be his father also taken captive many years previously.[28] A railway journey to London in *The Hypocrite* becomes the scene of equally fortuitous meetings.[29] In similar vein the fortunes of the heroes in the latter novel are redeemed by large and timely inheritances. Mapu seems to have been fascinated by large sums of money, which are repeatedly introduced into the plot.[30]

All three novels contain a strong admixture of dramatic irony, the source of which is twofold. The heroes frequently entrust their affairs to villains masquerading as honest and pious men. The consequences are, of course, disastrous. Both Amnon and Tamar, for instance, seek the help of Zimri, their bitterest enemy.[31] Similarly Jerahmeel endeavours to enlist Zadok's aid in his search for Hophni, unaware that Zadok is Hophni in disguise![32] The second source of dramatic irony consists in mistaken identity. Both Tamar and Teman suspect Amnon of having fallen in love with Teman's beloved, Peninah, in their ignorance of the fact that Amnon and Peninah are brother and sister.[33] Again Eliphelet, one of the heroes of *The Guilt of Samaria*, sees Eliada making love to his mother

26. Part I, ch. 2.
27. Part II, ch. 1.
28. *The Love of Zion*, ch. 26.
29. *The Hypocrite*, part IV, ch. 16.
30. Ibid., part II, chs. 6, 12 and 14; part IV, chs. 3, 9, 18 and 19.

31. *The Love of Zion*, chs. 19 and 20.
32. *The Hypocrite*, part II, ch. 12.
33. *The Love of Zion*, chs. 13 and 14.

Miriam, and is furious, not knowing that Eliada is really his father Uzziel.[34] The irony in every case is handled skilfully and is one of the more successful devices.

An ingredient common to all the stories is the frequent insertion of dreams and nightmares. In *The Love of Zion* the dream plays an important part in the plot:

> Towards evening on the seventh day the captivity reached the river Chabar, and there I ate the bread of affliction and slept upon the river's bank. And behold in my dream I saw a handsome youth in splendid raiment, girded with a sword and on his head the helmet of salvation. His brow was crowned with jet-black curls, his cheeks were rosy, his forehead soft as snow and fair as milk, and riding on a horse he appeared before me. And as I looked upon his splendid form I wept bitterly and cried: 'Alas, O God, I too had sons as fair as this youth, but not a single one remains to close my eyelids and inherit the fruits of my toil.' But when the youth heard my lament he alighted from his horse, clasped my right hand and said consolingly: 'I am he whose soul yearns for Tamar, the daughter of your daughter Tirzah; and I shall redeem you from the land of your captivity, and you shall return with me to Zion and your loved ones to rejoice there in God's light.' Then I asked him his name and family, but he replied: 'They must still remain secret, but in the course of years you shall know them.' Then he showed me the ring which I had given to Tamar and said: 'Here is the sign of the covenant which my beloved Tamar has given me.' At these words my heart leapt and I awoke—and behold, it was a dream, but a wonderful and precious dream in my time of grief and sorrow.[35]

In the other novels, too, dreams are frequently recounted or at least mentioned,[36] very often comprising interesting digressions

34. *The Guilt of Samaria*, part II, ch. 9.

35. *The Love of Zion*, ch. 3. See also ch. 27.

36. See *The Guilt of Samaria*, part I, chs. 5, 6, 8 and 16; part II, chs. 14 and 20. *The Hypocrite*, part II, chs. 2, 4, 9, 12 and 14; part III, chs. 2 and 13; part IV, chs. 1, 6, 9 and 10; part V, ch. 6.

from the main course of events. In this respect Levi's night-mare in *The Hypocrite*, in which he witnesses his own death and subsequent torments, is particularly fine.[37] Equally vivid in the same novel is Shubal's story of his nightmare, which has the additional moral purpose of emphasizing the need of faith in God.[38]

A further device, employed repeatedly in the stories, is the introduction of letters. They are used both for the advancement of the plot, and for purposes of description or reflection. Even in the historical novels their number is considerable, *The Love of Zion* containing six[39] and *The Guilt of Samaria* five.[40] They are treated as an everyday occurrence and occasion no surprise, in spite of the rare mention of letters in the Bible, and there almost always for state or other important correspondence.[41] *The Hypocrite*, however, includes more than sixty letters,[42] and contains features common to the class of epistolary novel exemplified by Richardson's *Pamela*. Frequently the letters serve to advance the plot in one of two ways. They may supply the reader with information not previously known or, by virtue of interception,[43] they may give the villains access to private details of their enemies, or afford an opportunity for forgery, thereby furthering their plans for the scandal, slander or persecution which comprise important factors in the plot. Often, however, they are used to interrupt the narrative at moments of tension, allowing the reader's emotions to subside in readiness for the next crisis. This device is far more successful. The letters from Palestine provide perhaps the most refreshing sections of the novel and are certainly the richest in des-cription.[44]

Among the more attractive techniques which Mapu em-

---

37. *The Hypocrite*, part III, ch. 2.
38. Ibid., part IV, ch. 10.
39. Chs. 3, 14, 15, 21, 23 and 28.
40. Part II, chs. 3, 5, 8 and 9.
41. See O. Eissfeldt, *Einleitung in das Alte Testament*, Tübingen, 1934, pp. 23 ff.
42. Part I, chs. 2, 3, 4, 5, 6, 7, 8, 10, 12, 13, and 14; part II, chs. 1, 2, 3, 4, 5, 6, 7, 8, 9, 10, 12 and 13; part III, chs. 1, 2, 3, 4, 7, 8, 9, 12 and 13; part IV, chs. 3, 4, 6, 7, 8, 9, 12 and 19; part V, ch. 4. See also below, pp. 55 and 102.
43. *The Hypocrite*, part I, ch. 12; part II, chs. 4 and 12; part III, ch. 7.

ploys, the minor stories interspersed in the novels figure prominently. In spite of the naïve and rather crude construction of the overall plots, the handling of the minor themes is skilful and delicate. Uzziel's story, for example, bridges a difficult time gap in outlining the events prior to the opening of *The Guilt of Samaria*.[45] Again the love story of Azriel and Shiphrah infuses an idyllic element into the rather sombre texture of *The Hypocrite*.[46] The minor episodes often demonstrate a vitality not found in the overall plots. In the historical novels, particularly, they provide much swift and dramatic action. Mapu is at his best in presenting a series of vivid pictures with all the brevity and pungency of Biblical narrative, and from time to time displays genuine touches of dramatic skill. Tamar, for example, wildly excited at hearing her lover's voice after a long separation, and anxious to run out to meet him, cannot find the key to her room.[47] Moreover the incidental description, such as the picture in *The Guilt of Samaria* of Jerusalem in mourning,[48] is of a very high order. This latter scene contrasts strongly with the unconvincing attempts in *The Hypocrite* to portray Hamburg[49] and London.[50] Apparently Mapu felt more at home in the capital of ancient Judah than in the great cities of contemporary Europe.

One additional feature deserves attention in *The Guilt of Samaria* and *The Hypocrite*. In the historical novel characters from *The Love of Zion* are frequently mentioned and even re-introduced.[51] The most notable example is the villain Zimri, who plays a leading part in both stories. Towards the end of *The Guilt of Samaria* he completely disappears from the stage. Mapu was faced with the difficulty of preserving him from the fate of his partners in crime, to fulfil his later adventures already described in *The Love of Zion*. Hepher, Bukkiah and

---

44. Ibid., part II, chs. 8 and 9; part III, chs. 12 and 13; part IV, ch. 8. See below, pp. 160 ff.

45. Part I, chs. 2 and 4.

46. Part II, chs. 8 and 9; part III, chs. 12 and 13; part IV, ch. 8.

47. *The Love of Zion*, ch. 29.

48. Part I, ch. 10.

49. Part IV, ch. 15.

50. Part IV, ch. 18.

51. *The Guilt of Samaria*, part I, chs. 1, 6 and 12; part II, chs. 2 and 12.

Carmi escape retribution on similar grounds. But even in *The Hypocrite* frequent reference is made to *The Love of Zion*.[52] The author was anxious to keep his first and most popular novel constantly before the public eye and lost no opportunity of stressing its worth.

The significance of Mapu's novels, however, stems less from the plots than from the glimpses they reveal of the life of two distinct eras. His strength lies in the sympathetic feeling for environment and atmosphere which permeates his stories. If it is the function of the novelist '. . . to reveal the hidden life at its source . . .'[53] or if the power of the artist is '. . . to guess the unseen from the seen, to trace the implication of things, to judge the whole piece by the pattern, the condition of feeling life in general so completely that you are well on your way to knowing any particular corner of it . . .'[54] then Mapu may be credited, at least, with having made an initial and not unimportant advance towards the fulfilment of that aim. For in *The Hypocrite* he has drawn a revealing, if limited, portrait of the life and values of his own society, while in the historical novels he has attempted to broaden and enrich the picture of a life presented by the Bible only in bare outline.

52. Part I, chs. 12, 13 and 14; part II, ch. 4.

53. E. M. Forster, *Aspects of the Novel*, p. 66.

54. Henry James, *The Art of Fiction*, New York, 1948, p. 11.

ANCIENT AND MODERN
SETTINGS

WHILE the plots of Mapu's novels are distinguished neither by originality nor by variety, his portrayal of setting is of a very different calibre. In all three novels the setting not only serves as a framework for the plot, but frequently usurps the interest and casts its own radiance over the darker patches of the stories. The plots may wear too thin, the characters may sometimes appear shadowy and unsatisfying, but the setting succeeds in maintaining its freshness of appeal. It has a life and virility of its own, and forms the stem from which the other branches of the novel grow organically.

In the measure that great novelists completely sum up a period by an evaluation of the forces at work in the society they depict, Mapu's writings are distinguished by his ability to bring an epoch to life. Inferior in all other respects, his success in creating atmosphere in his historical novels gains him a place among the masters. The rich imagination of a true artist enabled him to crystallize the life and society of the Bible. The flimsiness of the materials at his disposal serves only to emphasize his achievement. From the books of *Kings*, *Chronicles* and *Isaiah* it was possible to extract an historical background, echoes of the pattern of society, hints of dress and habits, but the spirit of life could be breathed only from his own nostrils.[1]

A significant pointer to the resource which Mapu displayed in expanding the outline history of the Bible may be found in the list of characters preceding *The Guilt of Samaria*.[2] The persons in the story are grouped according to families, and appended to the family of Zichri is the quotation:

And Zichri, a mighty man of Ephraim, slew Maaseiah, the king's son, and Azrikam the governor of the house, and Elkanah *that was* next to the king.[3]

1. Cf. A. Sha'anan, *'Iyyunim be-Sifrut ha-Haskalah*, p. 163.

2. *Mapu*, p. 72.

3. *2 Chronicles*, xxviii. 7.

From this slender evidence, Mapu constructed one of the principal themes of his plot. Not only does Zichri become an important character in the story, but in addition Mapu endows the slaughtered Elkanah with two wives, Jehosheba and Noah, and two daughters, Kezia and Shulamit, of whom all but Noah play leading roles throughout the drama. The scattered references of the Bible, pregnant with possibilities, afforded the ingredients which Mapu required. His strong imagination caught them up, clothing the bare bones with flesh and blood. The generous treatment of such isolated fragments of stories explains the secret of Mapu's creative force.

Mapu's real strength lies in his power of description, particularly the description of nature. His portraits of the scenes and landscapes of the land of Israel are outstanding. Living in the totally different surroundings of Lithuania,[4] Mapu accomplished the remarkable feat of conjuring up a vivid and convincing picture of a country he had never seen. Relying on his deep knowledge of the Hebrew Bible, which he exploited to the utmost, with perhaps the additional aid of a geographical work on Palestine by Jacob Kaplan, he visualized the hills and valleys, the towns and villages with an uncanny accuracy. That he made mistakes in geography is hardly surprising.[5] They may well be forgiven in the general completeness of the picture he presented. There can be no doubt that his novels stimulated in his readers a profound and detailed interest in the ancient homeland.

But Mapu did not confine himself to descriptions of the physical characteristics of the land of Israel. Even more significant is his portrayal of the pattern of life in Biblical times. It is of little importance that much of the incidental detail was supplied by his own fertile imagination. Unlike the historian, the writer of historical romances is not irritably bound by fact and detail. The spirit in this case is more important than the letter, and Mapu caught the spirit admirably. The vital currents of life emerge in a succession of vivid and brilliant scenes—the joy of

4. *The Love of Zion* was largely written in a pagoda on a hilltop near Kovno. See Brainin, op. cit., p. 32 f.

5. See *Klausner*, p. 338 f.

an abundant harvest;[6] the thronging crowds in Jerusalem for the Feast of Tabernacles;[7] the armed might and overweening pride of Nineveh.[8] Moreover the frequent interspersion of customs and beliefs echoed from the Bible constantly infuses touches of authenticity into the narrative. Naame, suspected of setting fire to Joram's house and therefore being responsible for Haggith's death, flees to escape the wrath of the avenging kinsmen.[9] Her supposed crime is then recorded by the elders at the gate.[10] Mattan suffers from the notion of the 'sins of the fathers':

And Ira said to Mattan: 'Behold! Your father crushed the poor and ground the needy, and upon you shall their curses descend. . . .'[11]

The nobles of Judah are roundly censured for wearing foreign-spun clothes.[12] Amnon swears a Nazirite oath to refrain from drinking wine:

And Amnon drank no wine, for he had vowed a Nazirite vow, to refrain from wine for thirty days on entering Jerusalem's gates.[13]

Nabal is handed over to his brothers for punishment:

. . . And he delivered Nabal to the sons of Achan, to do with him as they thought fit.[14]

The author desired to lose no opportunity of establishing a convincing background.

The plot of *The Love of Zion* is depicted in the southern kingdom of Judah, during the reigns of the kings Ahaz and Hezekiah. The story opens during the kingship of the former in a period of licentiousness and idolatry. But by the third

6. *The Love of Zion*, ch. 5.
7. Ibid., ch. 6.
8. Ibid., ch. 15.
9. Ibid., ch. 2.
10. Ibid.
11. Ibid., ch. 1. Cf. *Exodus*, xx. 5.
12. *The Love of Zion*, ch. 7.
13. Ibid., ch. 17.
14. Ibid., ch. 24.

chapter the scene has changed to the beneficent reign of Hezekiah, under whose guidance the evil practices of the former
king gradually disappear:

> The evil times had passed, and fathers no longer sacrificed
> their sons to Molech, and their daughters to an idol plated
> with gold and silver. . . .[15]

Mapu portrays the period as a 'golden age' for Judah. There is
a prophetic quality in the idealization of the period, as though
the author were wistfully projecting his ideal state into the past.
Righteousness, charity and prayer are the accepted standards of
good behaviour, and evil is compelled to work secretly and in
stealth:

> In the fourth year of the reign of Hezekiah, king of Judah,
> the evil of Ephraim reached its peak. And God in his wrath,
> after long anger at the sinful kingdom, brought upon her the
> avenging sword, the king of Assyria, who burst over the land
> like a mighty torrent, sweeping away the calves of the house
> of evil and the idols of Dan, and dragging off their wor-
> shippers, scattering them in Halah and Nabor by the river of
> Gozan and in the cities of the Medes. So Judah bestirred
> herself, seeing God's retribution and his punishment of her
> sister Israel, renewed her strength in her protector, and clung
> to the paths of the Lord, lending a willing ear to Hezekiah
> her king, the descendant of David and the beloved of God,
> who dwelled securely even while the land of Ephraim was
> overthrown. Wherefore his people remained faithful to
> him all the days of his reign.
> At that time a fugitive from the captivity of Ephraim
> reached the northern border of Zion, and casting his idol
> into a pit addressed it thus: 'Lie there in your shame, my
> wooden idol, for in the land of Judah you are an impotent
> god. These ten years I served you, carried you, endeared you,
> yea exalted you in the eyes of your worshippers. I cast your

15. *The Love of Zion*, ch. 10.

dread upon them and they feared you; I was your mouth, and you were my god. Together with the band of priests I murdered on the highways, yea I committed violence and oppression to my heart's desire, making your wish my pretext. I drank the wine of your oblations, and ate the flesh of your sacrifices; even the clothes upon my body came from you. How good those first days were, but evil times have come. Behold your foundations are destroyed, the calves of the house of evil are in exile, and whither shall you go? Shall I bear you to Zion? Will you not quake before the dread and mighty God that dwells in the midst thereof, and be a stumbling-block for me also? Therefore lie here, wooden idol, naked and ashamed. Give me your silver covering and garments of molten gold, for they cannot help or avail you aught, but they shall be my reward for serving you.'

Thus spoke the fugitive Zimri, one of the worthless, shifty priests of Baal, who used to throng the roads like brigands, preventing the men of Israel from going to Zion, to bow down to the Lord on the holy mountain. This Zimri had gone into exile with the captivity of Samaria, but being fleet of foot, he had escaped at the first opportunity, and knowing Hananeel, the nobleman of Samaria, he had asked from him the name of his son-in-law in Jerusalem. So he crossed the river Chebar and continued on his way. And Hananeel gave him a sealed letter and his seal to bring to Jedidiah his son-in-law. Now during his flight from the enemy, he had carried his idol with him all the way, thinking that he might find some place to set it up and serve it. But when he saw that in all the land of Judah no man turned to idols, he stripped it of its ornaments and cast it into a pit, and entered Jerusalem towards evening through the Samaritan gate. The city's streets hummed with noise, for people still thronged about thick as locusts; the elders sat reverently meting out justice at the gate, while litters and swift animals bore the chieftains and nobles of Judah to and fro in the streets. And Zimri, who for three years past had seen only the distress of siege inside Samaria's gates, while the king of

Assyria lay encamped over against her, was astounded by what he saw, and exclaimed: 'Samaria lies prostrated while Zion is elated! Samaria has been trodden down, while Zion rings with her king's renown! The land of Ephraim is plunged into despair, while the land of Judah blossoms fair. Lo! Here my eyes behold new heavens and new earth, a lovely earth, whose inhabitants dwell in peace; the pure heavens shower righteousness upon them from on high, for their king has proclaimed justice at the gate, and treads the way of truth. Verily, justice and righteousness are blessings for the rich, for they protect their wealth from hurt; but for a poor man such as I, whose livelihood has vanished, they are thorns upon the path—since Hezekiah has banished the Baals from his land. Yet who knows? Perhaps there are many here who still cherish their commandments. For what are the commandments of the Baals? Surely destruction and violence. And in what consists their worship? In plunder, oppression, murder and deceit. So then I shall search Jerusalem diligently till I find treacherous men—and what city is without them? Behold her rich are numerous, and they that envy them are legion. And if envy be joined to treachery, and treachery to energy, there shall the lord of the Baals emerge. And what need of images then? If only their true service be in our hearts, our lips, our hands, then shall the poor man rise from the gutter, and the lowly attain honour. Behold, righteousness is here enthroned, and justice dwells beside the gate. Wherefore I, too, shall gird my loins with righteousness to all appearances, but deceit shall inhabit the recesses of my heart; and with mealy mouth I shall cover up my schemings. Yea, I shall bend to the wind like a reed, while my lips utter pious sermons. For many prosper thus, and by their aid wax fat. For who is as blind as the servant of the Lord, or as deaf as the pure of heart? For such do not probe the thoughts of men or rightly consider whether the lips echo the real promptings of the heart, or whether the action suits the word. If only my deeds seem worthy, who will examine my innermost intent? Therefore let treachery only disguise herself in the robes of truth her adversary, and all that look upon her shall bow the knee.'[16]

Nevertheless in *The Love of Zion* the historical atmosphere is more in evidence than the historical events, which merely form a framework for the love theme of Amnon and Tamar, without dominating the scene. The only historical sequence of major importance is the threatened invasion from Assyria. The fear of approaching disaster is gradually developed,[17] even encroaching upon the boisterous conversation of the villains in Carmi's inn,[18] where Zimri gives a significant warning of the dangers of a war with Assyria. There is a quality of realism in this speech, which stands out in cold relief against the idyllic elements in the story. The threat culminates in the report that Sennacherib has crossed the Euphrates,[19] followed by the march of the Assyrians on Jerusalem.[20] Whereupon Ahaz rends his garments, Isaiah prophesies salvation and Jerusalem is miraculously delivered according to the Biblical narrative.[21] Mapu, however, expands the story, describing the amazement and joy of the population on seeing their enemy so utterly destroyed. Indulging in an additional item of historical fancy he pictures the surrounding nations recognizing the supremacy of the God of Israel.[22] Mapu was quite ready to supply events, where the Bible leaves so much unsaid. Although the results are sometimes a little far-fetched, his enthusiastic descriptions compensate in great measure for the lack of historical evidence.

Parallel with the historical background, a strong idyllic element runs through the story and pervades it with a sense of calm. Although a common ingredient of all Mapu's novels, in *The Love of Zion* it is particularly conspicuous. All three novels eulogize the delights of the simple, rustic life, and its superiority to the vice, bustle and restlessness of the city, in a manner worthy of Virgil's *Bucolics*.[23] All three employ the idyllic

16. Ibid., ch. 3.
17. Ibid., chs. 16 and 20.
18. Ibid., ch. 16.
19. Ibid., ch. 24.
20. Ibid., ch. 25.

21. *2 Kings*, xix.
22. *The Love of Zion*, ch. 27.
23. See particularly ibid., ch. 7, and *The Hypocrite*, part V, ch. 7. Cf. below, pp. 55 and 94.

device of soliloquy—in *The Hypocrite* it appears principally in letter form[24]—for the expression of contemplative calm or the speaker's reaction to the beauties of nature.[25] The nature portrayed is, of course, perpetually friendly, providing sustenance of itself, as seen through the eyes of the city-dweller, and not of the farmer, more familiar with its vicissitudes: nature, in short, as it appeared to the English romantic poets.[26] And all three portray a highly stylized version of romantic love, undying and faithful, despite every adverse trick of fortune—a love, too, frequently engendered at first sight, and in most unlikely circumstances.[27]

But whereas in the later novels the idyllic theme is a minor element, in *The Love of Zion* it is all-pervading, and lends its specific colouring to the whole novel.[28] In *The Guilt of Samaria* and *The Hypocrite* far greater importance must be attached to the historical and contemporary scene respectively, as the background on which the plot is embroidered, and the characters introduced. In *The Love of Zion* the love of Amnon and Tamar is paramount, and the historical setting, important as it is, remains secondary. In both the later novels the canvas is broader, and *The Guilt of Samaria* contains an element of epic.[29] *The Love of Zion*, on the other hand, is a microcosm, self-contained, and endowed with much of the sense of detachment and timelessness, so necessary for the idyll, which permeates, for example, Goethe's *Hermann und Dorothea*.

The idyllic romanticism of the love element, whose major motif is personified by Amnon and Tamar, is echoed also in the minor theme of the love of Teman and Peninah.[30] Tamar has fallen in love with a dream picture of Amnon, before she

---

24. See *The Hypocrite*, part II, ch. 9; part III, ch. 13.

25. *The Love of Zion*, ch. 29; *The Guilt of Samaria*, part I, ch. 16.

26. Cf. P. Laḥower, *Meḥḳarim we-Nisyonot*, Warsaw, 1925, p. 51.

27. Cf. *The Guilt of Samaria*, part I, ch. 4.

28. For a contrary view see *Klausner*, p. 336.

29. Cf. J. Fichman, *Anshei Besorah*, Tel-Aviv, 1938, p. 132. See also S. L. Ẕitron, *Yoẕerei ha-Sifrut ha-'Ibrit ha-Ḥadashah*, Vilna, 1922, p. 56.

30. During most of the story she is called Shoshana. See below, p. 127.

ever meets him in the flesh[31]—a love which Amnon returns at first sight. One glance is sufficient, too, for Teman to fall in love with Peninah.[32] Amnon and Tamar symbolize the story of poor boy and rich girl; with Teman and Peninah the combination is reversed. The fact that Amnon and Peninah are brother and sister, as are Teman and Tamar, completes this ideal balance. Amnon grows up a shepherd, and Peninah flowers into the full purity of her beauty in a poverty-stricken hut in the forest. Love first develops in the one case against a background of flocks of bleating sheep[33] and in the other a harvest festival.[34]

So strong is this pastoral, idyllic element that it finds expression in the oaths with which the characters pledge themselves. Naame swears Teman to secrecy with the words:

... I charge you by the roes, and by the hinds of the field. ...[35]

Amnon invokes the sun to witness his undying love, and Tamar calls upon the moon.[36] These oaths cannot be compared to the avowed idolatry so conspicuous in *The Guilt of Samaria*, where, for example, Keturah[37] swears frequently by her god, Chemosh,[38] for here an indictment of the idolatrous sins of Samaria is contained in the very title.[39] In *The Love of Zion* these oaths are put into the mouths of 'good'—and therefore righteous—characters, and represent an almost unconscious deference to pastoral idiom. This idiom reappears again and again, always with a most attractive freshness and simplicity, notably, for example, in the merry frolics of the grape harvesters,[40] or in the delicate touch, when Amnon and Tamar approach a stream from opposite sides, and their eyes meet

31. *The Love of Zion*, ch. 3.
32. Ibid., ch. 5.
33. Ibid., ch. 4.
34. Ibid., ch. 5.
35. Ibid., ch. 13. Cf. *Canticles*, iii. 5.
36. *The Love of Zion*, ch. 13, p. 35.
37. Notice the symbolism of the name Keturah (incense). For further remarks on Mapu's practice of employing symbolic names see below, p. 54.
38. Cf. part I, ch. 12, pp. 114 and 115.
39. Cf. *Amos*, viii. 14.
40. *The Love of Zion*, ch. 5.

only in the reflection of the water.[41] Indeed, these pastoral scenes, which afford such scope for calm, imaginative description and rich imagery, and where the background is so subtly reminiscent of the early stories of the Patriarchs, represent some of the most effective of Mapu's pictures.

Whereas in *The Love of Zion* the historical background serves only as a framework for the loves and intrigues of the individual characters, in *The Guilt of Samaria* it assumes much greater significance. Although the threads of the plot are far more numerous and entangled than in the first novel, and the tortuous relationships of the individual characters continue to occupy the centre of the stage, two deeper and more vital dramas are simultaneously enacted in the wings. On the one hand the national rivalries of Judah and Samaria portray the dark struggle for supremacy which continues throughout the story. On the other hand there is a constant and no less bitter fight between the worship of Baal and the faithful belief in God. These vertical and horizontal divisions, which split the national unity, indicate forces and realities which may be sought in vain within the complex of romantic entanglements, spidery intrigues and hair-breadth escapes of the heroes and villains. Judah and Samaria, Baal and Jehovah are the real forces in *The Guilt of Samaria*. Together with the characters proper they comprise a triple plane, which brings depth and perspective into the novel. The heroes and villains pirouette upon the scene like puppets whose strings are jerked by giant hands in the shadows. And in the background, like a lurking tiger, there is the constant menace of Assyria, threatening desolation and captivity.

The historical background of *The Guilt of Samaria* encompasses the kingdoms of Judah and Samaria in the last days of the latter. Most of the action takes place prior to the greater part of the story of *The Love of Zion*, but later than the first two chapters of the former work. It provides a natural prelude to Mapu's first novel, although the product of a considerably later period of the author's literary activity.[42] In consequence

41. *The Love of Zion*, ch. 4.   42. See above, pp. 21 ff.

the construction is more mature. Several of the characters of *The Love of Zion* reappear at a more youthful stage of development in *The Guilt of Samaria*, a factor which presented some intricate problems of integration. As they are mainly villains, Mapu had to resist the temptation to kill them off![43] The period comprises the dark days of the reign of Ahaz in Judah, and the happier period following the ascension of the righteous Hezekiah. In Samaria the story outlines the licentiousness and unbounded pride which dominated the reigns of the kings Pekah and Hoshen and culminated in the final catastrophe of the fall of the northern kingdom. The action revolves about the lamentable hatred of the two kingdoms for each other, the disastrous battle in which Judah is vanquished and Jerusalem overrun[44] and the disintegration of Samaria.

This broad background, which mirrors the ebb and flow of the tides of national fortune, adds an element of epic grandeur to *The Guilt of Samaria*, not felt in the earlier novel. The interweaving of personal and national issues, the exploits of kings and nobles, the admixture of prophecy and sacrifice all contribute to produce this effect. The most successful episodes in the story completely supersede the individuals involved. They consist in the vivid scenes of prisoners being led into captivity,[45] in the fine descriptions of the disastrous battle for Judah[46] or in the jostling, insulting crowds that flock to the celebration at the sanctuary at Beth-El which forms a prelude to the disaster that befalls Samaria:

> The mountains that enfold the sanctuaries of Beth-El re-echo noisily, and the altars of Baal tower in waves above the furrowed earth, for Ephraim has raised its sinful altars in abundance. The priests offer up their sacrifices, and the prophets of Baal caper round them like frenzied goats, cutting themselves, as is their custom, with spear and sword until the blood flows fast. For thus do they imagine in their folly that the divine spirit will descend upon them. And the

43. See above, p. 37 f.
44. Cf. *2 Kings*, xiv.

45. *The Guilt of Samaria*, part I, ch. 5.
46. Ibid., part I, chs. 8 and 9.

men and women of Ephraim feast and drink and sport upon the mountains, bellowing and inflamed with wine, their passions roused to fever heat. At their frenzy's height the youths and maidens all don masks, so disguising their features that none, neither man nor maid, may recognize his fellow. This, then, is the town Beth-El, from which the evil doctrine flows to every corner of the land.[47]

No less fine are the descriptions of the idolatrous spring festival in Edom,[48] or the gathering of the Ephraimite princes on the mountains of Samaria for sacrifice.[49] The old man who vainly urges the princes to return to Jerusalem and thus unify the nation arouses an echo of the Biblical narrative.[50] Throughout the story a constant denunciation is levelled against such abominable, idolatrous practices as human sacrifice to Molech.[51] The false priests and prophets of Baal, and their devices to mislead the common people, are similarly indicted.

Unlike the calm setting of *The Love of Zion*, the kaleidoscopic background of *The Guilt of Samaria* pulsates with movement and violent action. But in this story, too, there are many passages of natural description. The opening chapter of the novel, which introduces the lone bandit, dwelling on a mountain crag, has all the wild atmosphere of Walter Scott's *Peveril of the Peak*. Equally effective are the descriptions of sunrise on the mountains of Lebanon[52] and the portrayal of the fear and loneliness of a forest at night.[53] Here Mapu demonstrates once more that his main strength lies in description rather than action, in setting rather than plot.

In contrast to the depth and richness of the setting of *The Guilt of Samaria*, that of *The Hypocrite* appears shallow and pale. In spite of the great length of his novel on contemporary life, and the broad canvas on which it is portrayed—the scene swings from Lithuania to Macedonia, Italy, Germany, England

47. *The Guilt of Samaria*, part I, ch. 14. See also ch. 13.
48. Ibid., part II, ch. 11.
49. Ibid., part II, ch. 15.
50. Cf. *2 Chronicles*, xxx. 10.
51. *The Guilt of Samaria*, part I, ch. 6.
52. Ibid., part I, ch. 6.
53. Ibid., part I, ch. 16.

and Palestine—the pattern of life is nowhere profound. It remains true that Mapu succeeded in depicting the society with which he was familiar in considerable detail. But the life of that society was so hampered and restricted that its motivating forces appear comparatively trivial and petty. In place of human sacrifice and the worship of Baal, the evils to be over-come are hypocrisy and slander. In place of the disastrous, internecine strife between two kingdoms, both faced with complete destruction, the antagonism consists of wordy war-fare between orthodox and reform factions. The heroes are falsely accused of eating ritually unclean food[54] or selling ritually unclean wine.[55] Evil consists in the interception of letters[56] or the forging of credentials.[57] The pettiness of the issues reflects the shallowness of the life.

Nevertheless Mapu has etched a detailed picture of Jewish life in a small Lithuanian town in the last century. The novel constitutes an evaluation of what men lived by, their ideas and beliefs, their public and private relationships. It contains a veritable store-house of current folklore, superstition and local custom, including, for example, such medical practices as remedial blood-letting from the hand,[58] or visiting the graves of pious men in cases of sickness.[59] More importantly, the story depicts the bitter conflicts which divided the community into hostile factions, in particular the growing antagonism between the older generation, desperately anxious to preserve a rigidly traditional framework, and the younger generation thirsting after secular knowledge, frequently to the detriment of its loyalty to Judaism and the Hebrew language.[60] These conflicts, which served only to accelerate the powerful forces of dis-integration within Jewish life, were soon destined to result in revolutionary consequences of the utmost importance for subsequent Jewish history. The delineation of a social

54. *The Hypocrite*, part I, ch. 8.
55. Ibid., part IV, ch. 6.
56. See above, p. 32.
57. *The Hypocrite*, part II, ch. 4.

58. Ibid., part I, ch. 15; part II, ch. 1; cf. part II, ch. 14.
59. Ibid., part III, ch. 7.
60. Ibid., part II, chs. 2, 3; part IV, chs. 3 and 14.

background already in flux is indicative of Mapu's grasp of the problems of his own society.

In spite of the blatant melodrama and complex machinations of the plot, Mapu regarded his novel as a vehicle for serious social criticism. He was especially concerned with the inferiority of woman's status, and his heroines illustrate the changing relationship between the sexes in their striving for an adequate education and their hostility towards the accepted practice of arranged marriages irrespective of their own wishes.[61] Again, he was scathingly critical of a mental climate which demanded that Jews should deliberately remain in ignorance even of the language of the country in which they lived,[62] let alone of foreign languages, while at the same time blindly accepting what Mapu considered to be the irrational superstitions of the Ḥasidic sect.[63] That he described a world which has utterly disappeared only adds to the importance of the novel. It is significant, too, that the contemporary setting served as a model for Mapu's immediate successors almost without exception.[64]

His power of description, moreover, is as vivid here as elsewhere, whether in the atmosphere of poverty and despair that pervades Jeroham's household,[65] or in the overnight company of a wayside inn,[66] or in the delightful scenes contained in the letters from the Holy Land which rival the natural description found in the historical novels and form a connecting link between all his works. In The Hypocrite Mapu's skilful handling of the setting is once more in evidence. It suffers by comparison because the life portrayed is so shabby and drab. But that life represented Mapu's own world, and its portrayal serves only to emphasize the power of an imagination which could escape from it so utterly and reconstruct the world of the Bible with such colour and such conviction.

61. Ibid., part II, ch. 5; part III, ch. 1; cf. above, p. 15, below, pp. 61 and 95.

62. The Hypocrite, part I, ch. 12; part III, ch. 10.

63. Ibid., part III, chs. 2 and 12; part IV, ch. 16.

64. See below, p. 105 f.

65. The Hypocrite, part I, ch. 1.

66. Ibid., part I, ch. 9.

STUDIES IN BLACK
AND WHITE

IN spite of the differences in setting, chronology and subject-matter which sharply distinguish Mapu's historical romances from his contemporary social novel, an examination of the role of the characters reveals in either case the same twin features. On the one hand they represent little more than personifications of good or evil qualities, without depth or complexity. While their adventures may excite amazement, their personalities offer few occasions even for surprise. The subtle mystery which veils the innermost thoughts of the living person, the factor of unexpected reaction is almost entirely lacking. With few exceptions the whole personality is revealed to the reader, but rather as a pencil sketch than a portrait in oils. On the other hand the characters frequently appear to fulfil the part of observers, in which capacity they reflect the author's views on various aspects of society. In the manner of the Greek chorus they stand aside, approving or disapproving, but themselves taking little part in the main stream of action.

Both these phenomena stem from the tendentious nature of Mapu's writings,[1] and both are precedented in Hebrew literature. Mapu was familiar with the allegorical personification of virtue and vice, which appears in the dramas of Moses Ḥayyim Luzzatto (1707–47) and especially in his final drama *La-Yesharim Tehillah* (Praise to the Righteous).[2] Here the characters bear such names as Yosher (Righteousness), Emet (Truth), Tarmit (Falsehood) and Hamon (Populace), and roughly correspond with the personifications known as 'Humours' in English literature of the seventeenth century.[3] The people in Mapu's novels are, of course, more developed, and they are presented not as allegorical figures but real

1. See below, pp. 86 ff.
2. See S. Ginsburg, *The Life and Works of Moses Hayyim Luzzatto,* Philadelphia, 1931, pp. 109 ff. See also below, p. 100.

3. Cf. J. Palmer, *Ben Jonson,* London, 1934, p. 22.

persons.[4] They remain, nevertheless, more symbolic representations than individual personalities. Nor can it be a coincidence in *The Love of Zion* that the real name of the malignant yet foolish Azrikam is Nabal,[5] while the tavern-owner is appropriately dubbed Carmi.[6] Many such traces of personification occur throughout Mapu's novels. In *The Hypocrite* such names as Zadok, Gaal, Ahitub and Ahira are clear examples of this tendency.

Again the role of onlooker or *Zofeh* occupies an important place in the literature of *Haskalah*. The device stems from the picaresque story, whose object is '. . . to take a central figure through a succession of scenes, introduce a great number of characters, and thus build up a picture of society'.[7] In medieval Hebrew literature the great exponent of the picaresque story is Al-Ḥarizi (1165–1225), whose most important work *Taḥkemoni* is an imitation of the *Maqamas* of the Arabic writer Al-Ḥariri (1054–1121).[8] In European literature similar tendencies may be discerned in the epistolary fiction composed in the style of both Montesquieu's *Persian Letters* and Richardson's *Pamela*. The exponents of *Haskalah* adopted the framework, but used it polemically. In the two works *Megalleh Ṭemirin* (The Revealer of Secrets) and *Boḥan Ẓaddik* (The Touchstone of the Righteous) Joseph Perl (1773–1839) employs this method to pour ridicule on the *Ḥasidim* and to suggest remedies for the plight of Galician Jewry.[9] A similar social motive characterizes *Ha-Zofeh le-Beit-Yisrael* (The Watchman of the House of Israel) by Isaac Erter (1792–1851),[10] in which the emphasis on the observer is incorporated in the title. This work, published posthumously, comprises a collection of

4. Almost all the characters in Mapu's novels bear names derived from the Bible.

5. Cf. the Hebrew *Nabal* (to be foolish).

6. Cf. the Hebrew *Kerem* (vineyard).

7. E. Muir, *The Structure of the Novel*, p. 32.

8. See, e.g., M. Waxman, *A History of Jewish Literature*, New York, Vol. I, second edition, 1938, pp. 466 ff.

9. See S. Werses in *Tarbiz*, Vol. 31, No. 4, 1962, and D. Patterson in *The Annual of Leeds University Oriental Society*, Vol. IV, 1964.

10. Waxman, op. cit., III, pp. 188 ff.

articles and sketches, of which perhaps the most effective is the picaresque phantasy *Gilgul Nefesh* (Transmigration of the Soul). The device affords wide scope for the satirist and reformer.

While deviating from the strict form of his predecessors, Mapu has retained certain features of this technique. The process may be recognized most clearly in *The Hypocrite*, where the background of contemporary society is not unlike that portrayed by Perl and Erter. The observation, however, is no longer confined to the central figure, but diffused over a number of characters. Their function, moreover, is not restricted solely to that purpose, for they are sometimes involved in the plot, either by active intervention as in the case of Saul, or—as in Nehemiah's case—by virtue of the spiritual influence they exert on the other characters. A strong element of satire lurks in Saul's reflections and comments while reading the secret documents—the *Bat Ḳol*—of the marriage-broker Nahshon.[11] Ideas on social reform are contained in Nehemiah's long speech on the joys of country life.[12] This sentiment is immediately endorsed by Asaph, the writer, whose part in the plot is also confined to observation.[13] It is significant that although Nehemiah, who personifies the ideal *Maskil*, is constantly referred to, his actual appearance in the story is extremely rare. He is, however, the recognized champion of the principles in which the good characters believe, a fact which Ahitub, his son, very clearly acknowledges.[14]

The suitability of the letter for reflections on and criticism of the state of society is adequately demonstrated by Goldsmith's *Citizen of the World*. Similarly, the large number of letters in *The Hypocrite* provides a convenient medium for the expression of Mapu's ideas.[15] The character who composes the letter is able to advocate reform and reveal the evils of society, while

11. *The Hypocrite*, part I, ch. 9. Cf. below, p. 94f.

12. Ibid., part V, ch. 7. Cf. above, p. 45, below, p. 94.

13. *The Hypocrite*, part V, ch. 7.

14. Ibid., part I, ch. 5. See below, p. 89.

15. Cf. above, p. 36, and below, p. 102.

himself remaining little more than a shadow.[16] But the composer may also be a central figure in the plot who stands aside for a moment to present the author's ideas.[17] A similar tendency may be discerned even in the historical novels, in Amnon's letter from Babylon[18] and Jehosheba's letter to Miriam.[19] For although the contemporary novel offers much greater scope for didactic observation, frequent instances occur in *The Love of Zion* and *The Guilt of Samaria*. In the former Amnon is both central figure and prime observer, presenting Mapu's views in his summary of Isaiah's teachings,[20] in his exposition on correct conduct[21] and in his moving soliloquy on the love of Zion.[22] Indeed, Mapu constantly projects the ideals of the movement of *Haskalah* back into Biblical times. The same device of soliloquy is employed in *The Guilt of Samaria*. Shulamit's prayer echoes a deep faith in God,[23] a faith confirmed by Uzziel in his attack on the prevailing idolatry.[24] Uzziel performs the same dual role as Amnon, indicting the evils of his generation,[25] emphasizing the love of Zion[26] and pleading for the unity of the nation.[27] A central figure in the plot, he is yet capable of observing the weaknesses of the society in which he moves.

The didactic elements outlined above, however, are largely responsible for the weakness of Mapu's characterizations. Tendentious writing is not conducive to the broadest views; on the contrary it is apt to ignore the mixture of virtue and vice which comprises human character. The heroes in Mapu's novels embody the ideals of *Haskalah*,[28] while the villains

16. See Ahitub's letters, *The Hypocrite*, part I, ch. 5; part II, ch. 3. Also Asaph's letter, part IV, ch. 12.

17. See Elishebah's letter, ibid., part I, ch. 12. Also Naaman's letter, part I, chs. 13 and 14.

18. *The Love of Zion*, ch. 15.

19. *The Guilt of Samaria*, part II, ch. 3.

20. *The Love of Zion*, ch. 8.

21. Ibid., ch. 9.

22. Ibid., ch. 29.

23. *The Guilt of Samaria*, part I, ch. 16.

24. Ibid., part I, ch. 1. See below, p. 143.

25. *The Guilt of Samaria*, part I, ch. 7; part II, ch. 14.

26. Ibid., part II, ch. 5.

27. Ibid., part II, ch. 18.

28. See below, p. 86.

personify their antithesis. The characters are painted black or white, with hardly a trace of grey. Believing in the efficacy of direct example, Mapu portrays good men and bad men, carefully avoiding the more usual but, for the reformer, irritating inhabitant of the no-man's-land between. Didactically this method contains one great advantage, for the reader can entertain no doubts of the final supremacy of right over wrong. Artistically, however, it is less successful. As the virtues and vices portrayed are congenital, the bad characters are fundamentally, if uncomfortably, incorrigible. Thus the death-bed repentance of so many of Mapu's villains is artificial and unconvincing.[29] On the other hand the exaggerated morality of most of the heroes has a tendency to cloy. Both extremes serve only to emphasize the naïveté of the characterizations. In this respect Mapu's technique does not develop and in all three novels the pattern remains the same. The forces of evil, armed with treachery, hypocrisy and deceit, are finally overcome within an ace of victory by the powers of truth, virtue and enlightenment. The personification of the latter qualities falls into the category of *Maskil*.[30]

It has been suggested that the characters of a novel may be designated either 'flat' or 'round'.[31] The latter are many-sided creations, more representative of the varying facets of real human beings, while the former are constructed round a single idea or quality. 'The test of a round character is whether it is capable of surprising in a convincing way. If it never surprises, it is flat.'[32] By this definition most of Mapu's characters belong to the latter category.[33] The characteristics of the heroes are merely the various facets of the ideal *Maskil*. There is little essential difference between Amnon in *The Love of Zion*, Eliphelet in *The Guilt of Samaria* or Naaman in *The Hypocrite*. The same is largely true of Tamar, Kezia and Elisheba, respectively, although the latter is endowed with sharper intellectual

29. Cf. *The Love of Zion*, ch. 24.
30. See below, p. 90 f.
31. E. M. Forster, *Aspects of the Novel*, p. 93.

32. Ibid., p. 106.
33. This aspect is accentuated by the stilted dialogue. See below, p. 82 f.

faculties and a more independent spirit. The villains, in their turn, are equally representative of the opposite ideal. Zimri and Omri in the historical novels correspond to Zadok in *The Hypocrite* in hypocrisy, machination and unscrupulous behaviour. The broad canvas of the latter novel, however, afforded the author sufficient scope for a more detailed representation of the forces of decay at work within his own society. Apart from the hypocrite (Zadok) Mapu symbolizes the ignorant and unscrupulous upstart (Gaal); the religious bigot (Gaddiel); the respected but gullible citizen, duped by the hypocrites (Obadiah); and the pious 'good for nothing', learned, but unable to support himself materially (Jerahmeel).[34]

With few exceptions, therefore, the characters are less individuals than symbols, representing an unnatural concentration of virtue or vice. Only on rare occasions does the stress of long suffering broaden and deepen a character, and give it something of the spirit of life. In *The Guilt of Samaria* Uzziel and Jehosheba stand out as more mature and rounded figures. It is significant that in both examples the character is not entirely virtuous: Uzziel admits to having acted as a spy in his youth,[35] while Jehosheba bitterly regrets her former pride, which brought affliction on Noah and her daughter Shulamit.[36] The element of human weakness adds conviction to the strength of character both portray.

The merits of Mapu's creations must be sought, then, not as individual personalities, but rather in the possibilities of character which he presents. The writers of *Haskalah* were faced with a formidable obstacle in using the great figures of the Bible as heroes in their own works. They are portrayed so much better in the original form of the Bible itself.[37] In both *The Love of Zion* and *The Guilt of Samaria* Mapu's heroes are 'Biblical men', but not historical figures. He painted a new Jew, not a product of the diaspora but native to the soil of

34. Cf. *Klausner*, p. 346.

35. *The Guilt of Samaria*, part I, ch. 3.

36. Ibid., part I, ch. 6. Cf. below, p. 93.

37. Cf. J. Fichman, *Anshei Besorah*, p. 97.

ancient Israel. Within the limits imposed by the idealization
described above this new creation is vigorous and fresh, and
presents a healthy contrast to the stunted characters of contemporary Hebrew prose. The general treatment of the latter
has been summarized as follows:

> To sum up, Haskalah prose aspires to the same ideal Jew
> as does the poetry. But Haskalah poetry celebrates this ideal
> character as if he already existed. The prose treatment of the
> theme, by contrast, is sadly sober, even embittered by the
> realization of the great distance between the Jew as he is and
> the Jew as he should be.[38]

The Biblical setting of the historical novels allowed Mapu to
escape the dilemma. He was able to portray the Jew as he
should be by depicting the ideal Jew as he was.

Mapu does, however, introduce Biblical figures side by side
with his own creations, perhaps following the example of
Alexandre Dumas in *Les Trois Mousquetaires*, in which historical
figures appear together with the author's inventions.[39] In *The
Love of Zion* Isaiah and King Hezekiah appear in person during
the Assyrian attack on Jerusalem.[40] In *The Guilt of Samaria*
Ahaz, Hezekiah, Isaiah and Micah are introduced quite frequently.[41] Ahaz is even described as being in love with Miriam,
one of the heroines![42] Mapu undoubtedly exercised considerable daring in introducing prophetic figures and making them
perform upon his stage.[43] Although the prophets add little to
the plot, and although Mapu wisely refrains from any attempt
at detailed description, they help to establish authenticity of

38. S. Halkin, *Modern Hebrew
Literature*, New York, 1950, p. 52.

39. See A. Sha'anan, '*Iyyunim be-
Sifrut ha-Haskalah*, p. 164. See below,
p. 103.

40. *The Love of Zion*, ch. 27.

41. *The Guilt of Samaria*, part I,
ch. 3; part II, chs. 13 and 20.

42. Ibid., part I, ch. 3.

43. See *Klausner*, p. 341. Klausner

seems to have made an error, however, in confining these appearances
to *The Guilt of Samaria*: '. . . While in
The Love of Zion although the words
of Micah and Isaiah are given *in reported speech*, they themselves do not
appear upon the stage. . . .' Isaiah,
however, does appear and makes a
speech in *The Love of Zion*, ch. 27,
p. 62.

atmosphere and their speeches embody the ideals for which the heroes strive.[44]

Of the two broad classes into which the characters may be divided, the villains are the more convincing.[45] In spite of the exaggeration inherent in the author's method, they have a quality of realism and vitality largely lacking in the heroes. They are ruthless, resourceful and cunning, outwitting their opponents at almost every turn. When they enter the scene the stories quicken pace.[46] Mapu has endowed his principal villains Zimri, Omri and Zadok, with a malignancy akin to that of Iago. Their personalities suggest power and determination, and they display a sense of purpose which gives them life. It is they who set the plots in motion, and they who clearly know what they want. The heroes tend to be the objects rather than the subjects of the action, and their victories, especially in The Hypocrite, are due rather to devices such as sudden inheritances than determined action. Sometimes they display an annoying helplessness. When Uzziel, alias Eliada, learns of Shulamit's disappearance, he guesses correctly that she has been kidnapped, but can suggest no plan of rescue.[47] In face of the abduction of Ada, Zephaniah is equally unresourceful.[48] In contrast even the minor villains display a spark of life. They have a rough humour and carefree attitude, together with an exuberant appreciation of the pleasures of drinking. Hepher, Bukkiah and Carmi make an entertaining trio.[49]

Just as the villains tend to be more convincing than the heroes, the female characters are more skilfully portrayed than their male counterparts. Throughout his stories Mapu displays a delicate feeling for womanly emotion. All his young heroines are faithful, devoted and compassionate, while remaining spirited and independent. In The Hypocrite Elisheba represents

44. See The Guilt of Samaria, part II, chs. 13 and 20.

45. Cf. S. L. Żitron, Yoẓerei ha-Sifrut ha-ʻIbrit ha-Ḥadashah, p. 65 f.; J. Fichman, Anshei Besorah, p. 126.

46. Cf. The Love of Zion, ch. 16; The Guilt of Samaria, part II, ch. 10.

47. Ibid., part II, ch. 14.

48. Ibid., part I, ch. 5.

49. The Love of Zion, ch. 16.

Mapu's ideal conception of the new Jewish woman, devoted to her people, faith and language, but nevertheless determined to pursue her education and live a full and cultured life.[50] She presents a sympathetic but courageous figure, personifying Mapu's desire to foster the emancipation of the Jewish woman and raise her dignity and status. Even more successful are the portraits of the more matronly Miriam and Jehosheba in *The Guilt of Samaria*. Refined, wealthy and mellowed by suffering, they reflect a maturity and understanding rare in Mapu's characterizations. Expressive of Miriam's generous nature is her gracious consent to her husband's proposal to take the unhappy Jehosheba into his home as a second wife.[51]

But the heroines, too, have their wicked counterparts. The Amazon-like Keturah and her daughter, Reumah, clad in armour and breathing fire gallop on and off the stage. Reminiscent of Camilla in Virgil's *Aeneid*, these warlike women, terrible and cruel, present a strange, new spectacle in Hebrew literature. The scenes in which Daniel accepts Reumah's challenge to single combat are among the finest of all three novels.[52] In *The Hypocrite* female villainy is represented by Zaphnath. Lascivious, deceitful and fickle, she, too, is a character of flesh and blood, although the attempt to describe her womanly wiles sometimes finds the author a little out of his depth.[53]

Of the large number of persons who thread their way through the labyrinth of *The Hypocrite* three very minor characters alone possess the genuine spirit of life, and all three are outlined in a few paragraphs. The excellent portrait of Asenath was early discerned.[54] The little hunchbacked lady combines a strange mixture of goodness, superstition and prejudice which cloaks her with an individuality unusual in Mapu's novels. Equally vivid are two male characters, both

50. See above, p. 52, below, p. 95.
51. *The Guilt of Samaria*, part II, ch. 19.
52. Ibid., part I, chs. 13, 14 and 15.
53. *The Hypocrite*, part I, ch. 8.

54. R. Brainin, *Abraham Mapu*, p. 148. He confines her role, however, to one chapter, part III, ch. 7, whereas she reappears later, part IV, ch. 6.

servants. The jovial, heavy-handed Pethahiah, uneducated but respecting learning, faithful if undiscriminating, unashamedly fond of the bottle, is down-to-earth and refreshingly natural.[55] Of very different calibre is the unfortunate Ezra.[56] Forced to serve the wicked Zaphnath in order to support his family, but possessed of a burning sense of righteousness that cannot countenance the evil perpetrated in her inn, he has the genuine elements of a tragic figure. In his bitter outburst, '. . . And so I must look upon evil . . . and be silent',[57] there is an intensity reminiscent of Hamlet's 'But break, my heart, for I must hold my tongue!'

It is perhaps ironical that the least convincing characterizations in Mapu's novels are those which lay closest to his heart. The new generation of enlightened young men, symbolized in *The Hypocrite* by Naaman, Hogeh and Ahitub, are colourless and unreal. In these young *Maskilim* Mapu strove to find the saviours of the Jewish people and the harbingers of a new and better life. But they are too abstract and indeterminate, too far removed from purposive or concerted action to be of great significance. Indeed, the harsh conditions of Jewish life allowed little real scope for the activities of the *Maskilim*.[58] The idea of Zionism, which was later to serve as a focal point for young idealists and provide a fruitful avenue for constructive work, had not yet been crystallized. In spite of all Mapu's efforts the heroes of *The Hypocrite* remain pale shadows, the unreal visions of a vanished world.

55. *The Hypocrite*, part II, ch. 12; part IV, ch. 6.

56. Ibid., part I, chs. 9 and 11.

57. Ibid., part I, ch. 9.

58. Cf. J. Klausner, *Yozerim u-Bonim*, p. 186.

A NEO-BIBLICAL STYLE

O F the many influences exerted upon Hebrew literature by
the rise of *Haskalah* in Germany during the last decades
of the eighteenth century,[1] its effect upon the literary style
adopted by the majority of Hebrew authors for almost a
hundred years proved most decisive. In attempting to reform
the system of Jewish education as a prerequisite to any real
participation in the broader life of western Europe, the
exponents of enlightenment staunchly advocated the cultiva-
tion of more highly refined modes of expression as an essential
step towards a higher level of aesthetic appreciation. This
latter goal, it was believed, would also result in an improvement of ethical standards, in accordance with current concepts
of the close connection existing between ethics and aesthetics.
To that end the *Maskilim* deliberately opted for a return to
Biblical Hebrew in place of the somewhat crude and crabbed
style of Rabbinical composition then generally in vogue.

By emphasizing the superiority of the language of the Bible,
and particularly its sublime poetry, the advocates of *Haskalah*
hoped to develop the aesthetic sense regarded as so necessary
for Jewish regeneration, and at the same time—with the aid
of Biblical imagery and metaphor—help to rekindle the interest in nature which had been crushed by generations of
ghetto life. They believed, moreover, that a renewed study
of the Bible would foster a sympathetic appreciation of a
more heroic age in Jewish history with all its emphasis on
political freedom—an important psychological factor in the
struggle for emancipation. As a champion of the ideals of
Haskalah, Abraham Mapu proved so devout an adherent of
its literary creed that he may well be regarded as its most con-
summate exponent.

The style of Mapu's novels, therefore, is of necessity pre-
conditioned. Its source lies in the self-imposed limitation of
modelling his work primarily upon the style and language of

1. See above, p. 5 f.

the Bible.[2] In the absence of any prior Hebrew novel to influence his choice of style, the predilection of the exponents of *Haskalah* for the purity of Biblical Hebrew inevitably determined his medium. Moreover, it is reasonable to concede that many of the elements essential for his creations were to be found in the Bible. The *Prophets*, *Psalms* and *Job* provided the materials for natural description; the *Song of Songs* furnished him with the raw materials of romantic love; the books of *Samuel* and *Kings* afforded a simple but powerful model for narrative, while the point of view of the Bible with its clear-cut distinction between right and wrong, good and evil, provided the mould from which the 'black and white' characters might be cast. Upon these basic elements Mapu directed the powerful beam of his imagination, harnessed to a highly developed faculty for creating historical atmosphere, and a most sensitive feeling for language. These are the raw ingredients of Mapu's novels to which he adhered with remarkable fidelity.

For his reading public, too, the adoption of such a method possessed an immediate advantage. Familiarity with the content, language and style of the Bible provided a natural bridge to this new, literary domain. The transition was so natural,[3] the framework so well remembered, that to many *The Love of Zion* appeared almost as an extension of the Bible itself, and young lovers began to call each other 'Amnon' and 'Tamar'.[4] It is unquestionable that his delightful use of Biblical language must have been one of the chief reasons for the popularity of his novels—his readers would have felt so much at

2. In his novel of contemporary life, *The Hypocrite*, Mapu deliberately makes frequent use of Mishnaic and Talmudic phrases, and indeed himself protests that Biblical Hebrew is not an adequate vehicle of expression for the modern novel. *Mapu*, p. 455 f. As S. L. Zitron amusingly points out, however, even this protest is couched in Biblical language, so deeply was Mapu rooted in that

medium, *Yoẓerei ha-Sifrut ha-'Ibrit ha-Ḥadashah*, pp. 73 ff. And see below, n. 32 and p. 75, p. 82 and p. 106.

3. For the popularity of *The Love of Zion* among eastern Jewry see A. Ya'ari, 'Abraham Mapu Bein Yehudei Areẓot ha-Mizraḥ' in *Mo'zenayim*, III, 1931/2, part 48, pp. 10–12.

4. R. Brainin, *Abraham Mapu*, p. 48.

home! Moreover, the consistent employment of Biblical language provides a large measure of artistic unity, which prevails in spite of the weakness and intricacies of the plots. The very first paragraph of *The Love of Zion* strikes the keynote, and the reader is at once transported into a Biblical setting, comparable to that of the Bible itself. The climate is convincing and the enchantment real:

In the days of Ahaz, king of Judah, there lived in Jerusalem a man whose name was Joram, the son of Abiezer a nobleman in Judah and captain of the host. He was possessed of fields and vineyards in Carmel and Sharon, and flocks of sheep and herds of cattle in Bethlehem, which is in Judah. And he was rich in gold and silver with fine and stately palaces. And he had two wives, the name of one was Haggith, the daughter of Ira, and the name of the other was Naame. And Joram loved Naame exceedingly, for she was comely. But Haggith, her adversary, envied her and vexed her sore, for Haggith had two sons, while Naame was without child. But Naame was pleasing both to look upon and in her ways. So Joram gave her a dwelling for herself, that Haggith, her adversary, might not afflict her. Now Achan was the steward of Joram's household, and to him Joram gave Helah to wife, who was the Canaanite handmaid of Haggith. Moreover Joram had a bosom-friend, whose name was Jedidiah the Generous, a descendant of the royal house of Judah. He was the ruler of the king's substance, a man greatly beloved, still young but rich withal, and a protector of the prophets, the disciples of the Lord. For he loved to hear their sweet lessons, and readily inclined his ear to their parables, and sustained them with his gifts; wherefore they called his name Jedidiah the Generous. Thus did Joram and Jedidiah shine forth like precious stones in that wicked generation, the generation of Ahaz, for they were faithful to the Lord and to his holy ones. And they walked with the Lord's disciples, who clung fast to Isaiah's teachings, and on whom the law of God was sealed.

But the premise that the linguistic foundations of *The Love of Zion*, *The Guilt of Samaria* and in great measure *The Hypocrite* are Biblical is in itself a striking reflection of Mapu's creative powers. The initial problems facing the author in this choice of medium were as difficult as they were obvious. How could Biblical language adequately satisfy the very different demands of the novel? How could words and phrases, sanctified by religion and made authoritative by thousands of years of tradition, be adapted to a secular and fictitious context? Finally—and perhaps most seriously of all—how could such usage fail to suffer by comparison with the unassailable grandeur of the original? Each formidable in itself, the three problems together formed a seemingly insuperable obstacle.

The strength of Biblical narrative lies, moreover, in the brevity of the stories. Its adaptation for the purposes of a full-length novel confronted the author with the very serious problem of maintaining the interest over long periods in a medium especially suited to conciseness of expression. Mapu was compelled to paint atmosphere and create detail, while using a Biblical style which concentrates only on essentials. The sublimity of Biblical narrative arises from the restraint displayed at moments of great dramatic tension. At such moments, when an explanation might destroy the entire effect, a terse phrase can arouse the deepest emotion. Such is the force of Abraham's answer when Isaac seeks the victim for sacrifice.[5] Herein lies the poignancy of the description of the dead concubine with her hands upon the threshold.[6] The imagination is inflamed to the point of outrage, yet in the first example the Hebrew uses six words and in the second example three.

The Bible story is characterized by a hardness of outline, by a rigid economy of expression, by a relentless exposition of consecutive facts, with almost no attempt at psychological analysis or philosophic speculation which may serve as motivation. Thus the early life of Moses to the time of his selection for the divine mission is sketched in a few, brief pictures.[7] The

5. *Genesis*, xxii. 8.
6. *Judges*, xix. 27.
7. *Exodus*, ii.

significant facts are singled out and hammered home. All extraneous detail is ignored, or left to the reader to supply. The Bible story is a narrative of events arranged in their time sequence. It is a skeleton narrative that bites into the imagination to supply the flesh and blood, and therein lies its strength.

But as E. M. Forster has observed: '. . . there seems something else in life beside time, something which may conveniently be called "value", something which is measured not by minutes or hours, but by intensity . . . And what the entire novel does—if it is a good novel—is to include the life by values as well. . . .' [8] And again: '. . . but observe already how that other life—the life by value—presses against the novel from all sides, how it is ready to fill and indeed distort it, offering it people, plots, fantasies, views of the universe, anything except this constant "and then . . . and then . . ."'.[9] As a novelist Mapu had to supply those very elements of 'value' which Biblical narrative is so careful to omit, while at the same time using a medium of expression which derives its force from such omission. It is hardly surprising that he sometimes fails badly; it is all the more surprising that he has achieved so large a measure of success.

Mapu's answer to these problems consisted of a direct attack upon his material, without reservation and without apology. The Bible in its entirety became grist for the mill of his invention. Complete appropriation was followed by analysis and refashioning. The ingredients remained, but the treatment was varied at need. The emergent pattern retained much of its original colouring, entire phrases and suitable images being introduced unaltered, or slightly modified for the new situations. But more often the reshuffling amounted to a new creation, without losing the spirit of the original. If the final result had not the sublimity of the Bible, it was nevertheless inspired. Although the peaks could not be reached, a very high general level was achieved. With the dangers of plagiarism and parody confronting him at every step, Mapu succeeded in threading his way to the height of originality. That he has

8. *Aspects of the Novel*, p. 44 f.   9. Ibid., p. 60.

had no successors, in spite of the popularity of his novels, is ample testimony of the difficulties that beset the way.[10]

The authenticity of the Biblical scene, which forms the background of both Mapu's historical novels, is engendered by this constant and thoroughgoing employment of the characteristics of Biblical language. There is, indeed, an interpenetration of Biblical idiom which forges between these novels and the Bible a link so genuine and so organic that it is not without reason that they have been described as a new commentary on the Bible.[11] From the Biblical language stems the Biblical quality of setting, atmosphere, dialogue[12]—and hence characters—and even to some extent action.[13]

Mapu appears to have been so steeped in the language of the Bible that he thought in it and lived it—as though he had inherited the mould of thought of its ancient authors. His art resides in his ability to introduce Biblical phrases or adapt Biblical passages while preserving an impression of natural and organic expression. The appeal lies in the familiarity yet aptness of the transmutation. The well-known passage is adapted to serve a new purpose, without destroying the original spirit. Innumerable short snatches of phrase are drawn from the Bible either in their entirety or with a subtle modification, which leaves no doubt of their origin. Yet the Biblical association of such phrases inevitably reinforces their effect upon the reader.

The merit of such application must be sought in the delicate restraint which the author exercised. His prose does not glitter with Biblical gems, painstakingly quarried from the mine of the Bible, as is the case with so many of the writers of *Haskalah*. Only on rare occasions does a Biblical phrase project abruptly from his writing.[14] Close examination reveals his novels to be alive with the phrases of the Bible, but almost always so skil-

---

10. Cf. S. L. Zitron, op. cit., p. 82.

11. J. Fichman, *Anshei Besorah*, p. 94.

12. See below, pp. 78 ff.

13. For example, the powerful, dramatic embodiment of the phrase found in *Amos*, ii. 6: 'Because they sold the righteous for silver, and the poor for a pair of shoes.' See *The Guilt of Samaria*, part II, ch. 10, p. 167.

14. Notice, for example, the arti-

fully placed that the picture is clear, while the countless jigsaw pieces that comprise it remain invisible.

The danger that the method might produce a jumbled patchwork of Biblical phrases was always present. Every turn of phrase threatened distortion of context or interruption of the smooth course of narrative. His success consists in the fact that the attention is excited but not distracted. The reader is able to appreciate the Biblical allusion without being diverted from the story. Recognition is simple but not obvious. The phrases are clear, but they do not leap out of the text. Whether drawn directly from the Bible or original creation the language is subtly fused into a single harmony.

The fundamental mechanics of Mapu's prose constitute a fusion of elements of both the prose and poetry of the Hebrew Bible. From the prose he adopted the 'Waw Consecutive'—the phenomenon of Hebrew grammar that determines the swift-moving action, the relentless consecutiveness and the subtle colouring of Biblical narrative.[15] From the prose, too, he derived the terseness of outline, the bare yet rhythmic statement, the simple but significant phrase, and, above all, the economy of expression that, stripped of all unnecessary adornment and sometimes tantalizing in its austerity, can yet, with a few vivid strokes, sum up a whole period or—what is still more difficult—convincingly span a long passage of time. Thus the boyhood and youth of Azrikam, during which the evil growth of his character gradually festers through long years, is depicted in the single vivid sentence:

> And Azrikam grew up in Joram's house like a malignant thorn.[16]

But from the richer language of Biblical poetry he derived

---

ficial use of the following phrase modelled on *Job*, xxviii. 14: 'Ephraim saith, It is not in me: and Manasseh, It is not with me.' *The Guilt of Samaria*, part I, ch. 12, p. 115.

15. In the historical novels the 'Waw Consecutive' is an organic, and ever present element of the style. In *The Hypocrite* its use is sparing, and examples are comparatively rare.

16. *The Love of Zion*, ch. 3, p. 8. Cf. *Ezekiel*, xxviii. 24.

the materials necessary to bridge the gap between story and novel. The poetry of the Bible provided the pithy phrase, the forceful parallel, the penetrating contrast, and more especially the richness of imagery.[17] Therein lay the sources of natural description, ethical inspiration and idyllic love. In short it contained the living word, the key to conviction and reality. The very choice of Biblical theme and setting threatened at once both artificiality and imitation. Only by a fusion of the language of both poetry and prose could Mapu create a medium sufficiently flexible to overcome the difficulties inherent in his task. It is this which gives the singing cadence and lyric texture to his prose. But only a careful examination can reveal the thoroughness, the painstaking selection and combination of phrase, which underlies the apparent simplicity and the smooth current of his writing:

> So Daniel was left alone with Joach, who stood wrapped in thought with eyes fixed upon the smoke rising from the incense above the groves, while ideas welled up from the depths of his heart: I gaze at the earth beneath my feet, and raise my eyes to the heavens. I ask of you, great luminaries—sun, moon and stars. Who summoned you from the dark void? Who created you from nothing and set you there? You move along eternal paths, resting neither by day nor by night, but revolving ever more. If, then, you are gods, why do you not rest? Therefore you must be servants of the Almighty—and not gods. And so the heavens do proclaim. But when I look upon the earth the same thought arises. These groves, sacred unto the Ephraimites, deceive their worshippers. I hear the rustling of their branches, which seem to whisper softly: God hides himself. The secret of his power lies in the heavens, while the earth and all its host hears but an echo of his greatness. Therefore, great God, cast your spirit from on high upon these misguided people, that they may know their Creator.[18]

17. See E. König, 'Style of Scripture', in Hastings, *Dictionary of the Bible*, extra vol., 1904, pp. 156–69.

18. *The Guilt of Samaria*, part I, ch. 14.

It is true that Mapu, no less than other exponents of *Haskalah*, was obsessed by the principle of adherence to *Meliẓah*,[19] a concept which lays great emphasis on the choice and arrangement of words and phrases. At its best the term represents the sensitive selection of an apt and colourful image, particularly when drawn from the Bible. But it is an attitude to language which only too easily declines into high-flown and euphuistic expressions, sometimes bordering on the fantastic. All too frequently it is characterized by a mediocrity of subject matter swaddled in inflated and over-ambitious phraseology. For its adherents, however, *Meliẓah* symbolized 'good taste', suggesting a highly developed, aesthetic approach to life. Where Mapu differs from his fellow *Maskilim* is not in any underestimation of the importance of 'good taste'—indeed, this theme recurs constantly in his works[20]—but in the very fact that his own sense of 'good taste' is so highly developed. Hence it is that his ceaseless appropriation and adaptation of Biblical phraseology, often of the highest imaginative order, nevertheless mingle smoothly and imperceptibly with the texture of his own style.

As an illustration of the fine balance which time and again retains the flavour of the Bible, and which immediately arouses associations in the mind of the perceptive reader, a few examples may suffice. In her revulsion at the thought of an approaching union with the loathsome Azrikam, whose very presence she cannot bear, Tamar utters the half-prayer:

May He, who puts an end to darkness, put an end to Azrikam's love for me.[21]

Again, when Teman, while admitting the obscurity of Amnon's birth, nevertheless defends his beauty, wisdom and

---

19. The exponents of Enlightenment appear to have taken the derivation of this word from the Hebrew root *Malaẓ*, found only in *Psalms*, cxix. 103, meaning 'to be smooth', as applied to pleasant words. But see below, p. 88 f.

20. See below, pp. 88 ff.

21. *The Love of Zion*, ch. 6, p. 15. Cf. *Job*, xxviii. 3.

strength, Azrikam adapts a phrase from *Amos* into a biting retort:

> These three I can forgive him—Azrikam answered—but for the fourth, his learned tongue, I will not turn away the punishment.[22]

Both phrases evoke an immediate response as of something long-remembered, while fitting subtly into the framework of correct context. Indeed, a great part of the charm of Mapu's style is that the mind of the reader well versed in the Hebrew Bible—just as the 'Soul' in Socrates' 'Theory of Ideas'—seems little by little to remember and recognize scenes once perfectly familiar.

Frequently, moreover, a passage from the Bible is interpolated with slight modification, wherein the rhythmic parallelism adds an additional emphasis or poignancy to some moment of deep emotional stress. Stricken with pain and despair at what she considers unspeakable baseness in Amnon, Tamar bursts out:

> I cry unto the mountains, Cover me; and to the hills, Fall on me.[23]

On the other hand Mapu can employ the same device with equal facility to summarize background and create atmosphere, coining a parallel phrase scarcely distinguishable from the Bible itself. Thus he portrays a political background so corrupted that the righteous are forced to seek safety in concealment and flight with the words:

> Righteousness dwelt only in the forest, and Faith in caves.[24]

No less effective than the constantly recurring parallelism is the frequent use of contrast, which performs the same function

---

22. *The Love of Zion*, ch. 9, p. 25. Cf. *Amos*, ii.

23. *The Love of Zion*, ch. 22, p. 53. Cf. *Hosea*, x. 8.

24. *The Guilt of Samaria*, part I, ch. 1, p. 73. See below, p. 134.

of terse summarization, as, for example, when Uzziel expresses the bitter hopelessness of his position in the phrase:

Lo! My grief is close at hand, but help is far away.[25]

Even more poignant because of the play on words is Amnon's lament on the disastrous turn of events:

Tomorrow, which should bring me joy, comes to destroy. I hoped that day my bride to wed, not tears to shed.[26]

This trick of style, however, can easily be overplayed, and Mapu on occasion, although rarely, succumbs to the temptation of juggling with words to the detriment of the required emotional effect. Amnon, for example, expresses his unhappiness in phrases which tend to arouse amusement rather than pity:

. . . And affection has turned to rejection, kind looks to rebukes, fair-play to dismay and morning to mourning.[27]

Sometimes attention is focused on a particular point of interest by means of the strident call used in the prophetic books of the Bible. In the opening chapter of *The Guilt of Samaria*, a connecting link with the previous historical novel, *The Love of Zion*, is forged and the readers' attention immediately riveted by the line:

Do you not know, have you not heard how the noble Joram met his end . . .?[28]

Again a clearly Biblical note is sounded in the explanation of the significance of names given to many of the characters:

And she called her name Shulamit, saying: may the Lord grant me peace (Shalom).[29]

25. *The Guilt of Samaria*, part I, ch. 4, p. 90.
26. *The Love of Zion*, ch. 23, p. 55.
27. Ibid., ch. 26, p. 61.
28. *The Guilt of Samaria*, part I, ch. 1, p. 74. Cf. *Isaiah*, xl. 28. See below, p. 137.
29. *The Guilt of Samaria*, part I, ch. 2, p. 77. Cf. especially *Genesis*, xxx.

or again:

> My beloved son, Eliphelet, still lives, for you, O God,
> preserve him (Mefalleṭo). . . .[30]

The examples cited above constitute a few of the innumerable
phrases modelled on the Bible, and the many idiomatic devices
by means of which Mapu succeeds in creating the Biblical
framework and colouring of his historical novels. The style
constitutes the web and woof of his whole fabric. Without it
the entire conception, in spite of its setting in Biblical times
and in ancient Israel, and in spite of the introduction of
historical characters,[31] would remain hopelessly artificial and
unconvincing.

The extreme limitations of Biblical language naturally compelled Mapu to rely greatly on the *Hapax legomena*, and on the
rare words and combinations of words, which appear in the
Bible. He frequently modified the form of the word or phrase
to suit his own context, sometimes colouring the adaptation
with a new shade of meaning. In this respect, however, his
approach was generally cautious, calculated to ensure the aptness of any fresh connotation. On numerous occasions, however, Mapu became the inevitable, if unconscious, victim of his
own educational background. His deep and wide-ranging
familiarity with the vast corpus of post-Biblical literature frequently impelled him to introduce words and phrases endowed with shades of meaning not found in the Bible, but
firmly established in the later strata of the language.[32] Other
words, again, are employed with a connotation deriving from
their usage in Yiddish—Mapu's own vernacular. Frequently,
moreover, resort is made to vocabulary which does not occur
in the language of the Bible at all.

30. *The Guilt of Samaria*, part I,
ch. 8, p. 100.

31. See above, p. 59.

32. The subject is currently being
investigated by Mr. Y. Carmiel of
the University of Leeds in a disserta-
tion entitled: 'A philological examination of the post-Biblical vocabulary of Abraham Mapu's fictional
writings and a study of its sources,
with observations on its influence on
the development of Modern Hebrew'.

A parallel linguistic problem is reflected in another facet of Mapu's style. His writing shows a remarkable fondness for particular phrases, which he employs constantly.[33] The frequency of these phrases, which recur time after time throughout his novels, inevitably arrests the reader's attention. This phenomenon is partly due to Mapu's preference for *Melizah*. More importantly, however, it provides one of the clearest illustrations of the limitations of language at his disposal, which compelled him to resort repeatedly to the same expression. The problem is felt elsewhere. Purist as he was, Mapu was yet compelled to expand his linguistic resources more deliberately in the composition of *The Hypocrite* in order to find terminology suitable for the problems of contemporary life, for which Biblical Hebrew proved to be a clumsy and inadequate medium.[34]

In view of the arguments propounded above it must be stressed at this stage that *The Love of Zion* and *The Guilt of Samaria* are historical novels, but not Biblical novels. Mapu drew widely on the Bible for his style, language and setting, and these Biblical elements are fundamental in both novels. The fusion is so complete that from it arises the feeling of organic

---

33. These frequently recurring phrases are Biblical idioms, and serve to emphasize the ornate and poetic quality of Mapu's prose. A few typical examples, with the corresponding translation from the Authorized Version, may suffice to illustrate this feature of his style:

To express guilt
Hakkarat panaw 'anetah bo.—Cf. *Isaiah*, iii. 9. The shew of their countenance doth witness against them.

To express alarm
Libbo paḥad we-raḥab.—Cf. *Isaiah*, lx. 5. Thine heart shall fear, and be enlarged.

To express postponement
'Od ḥazon la-mo'ed.—Cf. *Habakkuk*, ii. 3. The vision is yet for an appointed time.

To express an aim
Maḥoz ḥefẓo.—Cf. *Psalms*, cvii. 30. Desired haven.

To express chagrin
Nasa besaro be-shinnaw.—Cf. *Job*, xiii. 14. Wherefore do I take my flesh in my teeth.

To express longing
Kol yish'o we-ḥefẓo.—Cf. *2 Samuel*, xxiii. 5. All my salvation and my desire.

34. Cf. *Klausner*, p. 350, and cf. above, p. 64, n. 2.

growth from the parent source. But the stories are not mere imitations of the Bible. No attempt has been made to expand either one or several of the Bible stories into novel-form. Nor can the prose, in spite of its Biblical elements, be equated with any particular sections of the Bible. Indeed, a careful analysis of Mapu's style reveals many syntactical idiosyncrasies, frequently resulting in types of sentence-structure unknown to Biblical Hebrew. Mapu's works depict the life and times of the Bible, and breathe much of its spirit, yet they remain unmistakably original creations.

Despite the element of swift-moving action, the melodramatic intrigues and desperate deeds, among which murder and arson figure prominently,[35] one of the most striking features of the historical novels is the calmness of the style. This phenomenon manifests itself partly as a dramatic technique. Mapu frequently opens his chapters with a passage of natural description, usually of great beauty, which at once provides a fixative and anchorage for the stories, rooting them deeply in the soil and landscape of the ancient land of Israel, and serves as a gentle spring-board for fresh developments in the plot.[36] The device is also frequently used to interrupt the narrative at moments of high tension, allowing the emotions to subside, while maintaining the reader in suspense. A notable example is contained in the fine description of the ox prepared for sacrifice in the temple at Jerusalem proudly conscious of the divine significance of his fate.[37]

But more especially this sense of calm is inherent in the idyllic element, which may be found in all three novels, but particularly in The Love of Zion.[38] The pastoral atmosphere and idyllic setting, with which Mapu endowed his first novel, together produce a sense of harmony and peace. The story unfolds smoothly, and even on the frequent occasions when violence or evil design or harsh war-trumpets burst dis-

---

35. See above, p. 33 f.

36. The Love of Zion, chs. 7, 22 and 23; The Guilt of Samaria, part I, ch. 7; part II, chs. 4, 12 and 14.

37. The Love of Zion, ch. 5, p. 13. Cf. Mishnah, Bikkurim, 3, 3. See below, p. 128.

38. See above, pp. 45 ff.

cordantly into the foreground, the ripples of sound soon subside into the calm surface of the narrative. The resulting
impression is one of completeness. The style glosses over the
sharp corners and rough improbabilities of the plot.

Thus it is that by virtue of its evenness of style and its unity
of artistry *The Love of Zion* represents the most complete
creation of all Mapu's novels. In *The Guilt of Samaria* he delved
far more deeply into Biblical history, and the work is far more
mature in the dramatic construction, the delineation of background and the realism of the evil forces embodied. In *The
Hypocrite* the contemporary scene is depicted in broad aspect,
and an attempt is made to sum up the life and values of the
author's own world. But the very length and scope of these
two novels throw up their faults into sharper relief. The course
of the narrative is not even, frequently the interest flags badly,
there is much doleful repetition, and very weak, flat passages
occur where the theme is stretched too thin. These faults are
inherent in the style. The effectiveness of the chosen medium
varies inversely with the length of the novel. *The Love of Zion*
is sufficiently short and concentrated to justify the use of a
Biblical style. As the length and complexity of the succeeding
novels develop, the inadequacy of such a style becomes
increasingly apparent.

IN SEARCH OF A VERNACULAR

O F all the difficulties with which the novelist is confronted, and which vary according to the nature of his theme and approach, the central problem of convincing dialogue remains constant. No matter whether the novel is primarily concerned with the portrayal of action or character, no matter whether its principal motivation is to point a moral or solely to amuse, the living word constitutes an indispensable instrument. The raw materials for the novel encompass almost the entire range of life itself, some part of which the novelist is always attempting to portray. But just as human speech is the underlying principle in all the manifestations of society, without which group life as a whole is inconceivable, so dialogue is the pivot about which the complex ingredients and relationships of the novel revolve. A novel, then, will be true to life and convincing in direct proportion to the sense of reality and conviction apparent in the dialogue. For whereas in real life the individual character creates and moulds his utterance, in the novel, by a reverse process, it is the dialogue which creates and moulds the characters. If the dialogue is natural and alive, the characters will follow suit. But if the dialogue is stilted and artificial, no descriptive power of the writer, however great, will bring the characters to life.

For the author writing in a living language the acquisition of the materials for dialogue presents no great problem; he has only to use his ears—even if the process demands eavesdropping on the conversation of chambermaids through a hole in the floorboards, as practised so successfully by the dramatist J. M. Synge. In his daily life and at every turn he is confronted with the unbounded richness and variety of human expression, which he may adopt, modify or imitate at will. For Mapu the problem was very different and far more difficult. He set out to write novels in a language which had not been used in common speech for tens of centuries. The language had indeed maintained an unbroken literary tradition of vast extent.

78

But even this literature was mainly concerned with religious, legal or legendary material, to the comparative neglect of matters more closely related to everyday conversation. In the virtual absence of a spoken idiom from which he might draw inspiration, this task must be regarded almost as a *creatio ex nihilo*, and represents one of Mapu's major contributions to the development both of Hebrew literature[1] and of the very conception that Hebrew might be revived as a spoken language. Even to the present generation, long familiar with the phenomenon of Hebrew as a natural and accepted instrument of daily speech, Mapu's success is impressive if somewhat quaint. To Mapu's contemporaries and near contemporaries the effect must have been startling, and the significance of the achievement clear.[2] It would be unfair to expect that at one fell swoop Mapu should forge an instrument sufficiently flexible to portray the infinite variety of expression required by the novelist to suit every conceivable time and situation. Mapu, clearly, could do no more than pave the way. The criterion for criticism in this instance must be that he succeeded at all—that the dialogue was actually written.

But Mapu was faced with an added difficulty. As his specific aim was to create a novel in the language of the Bible, he was compelled to renounce the characteristic language of subsequent strata of Hebrew literature, which would have rendered him invaluable assistance in the formation of dialogue. As if the difficulty of creating a living idiom from a literary language were not enough, he had in addition to confine himself to one section of that literature, a section, moreover, whose vocabulary is limited in the extreme.[3] Within the framework of this literature—the primary source upon which Mapu could draw—the passages couched in the form of conversation comprise a comparatively small proportion of the whole. Yet

1. Cf. below, p. 105. For even earlier attempts to foster a spoken idiom see C. Rabin, '*Ibrit Medubberet Lifenei 125 Shanah*, in the series *Leshonenu la-'Am*, Jerusalem, 1963.

2. Cf. R. Brainin, *Abraham Mapu*, ch. 18.

3. Less than six thousand different words according to *Gesenius' Hebrew Grammar*, § 2 *w*, n. 2.

from these flimsy materials Mapu succeeded in constructing the dialogue of two entire novels, together with by far the greater part of a third.

Interspersed in the Bible there are, of course, elements of dialogue full of the freshness and spontaneity of living speech, such as the conversations in the book of *Ruth* or those between God and Satan in *Job*[4] or the scene in which Solomon is confronted by two women, each claiming to be the mother of a child.[5] It has, indeed, been pointed out that Mapu was the first to make full use of these elements,[6] which were invaluable by virtue of their scarcity, and which had to be exploited to the maximum. But apart from these primary sources the Bible contains numerous secondary sources of dialogue, that is material which, although not in the actual form of conversation, can be adapted to dialogue quite naturally and with little alteration. Elements of dialogue lurk beneath the surface of the numerous stories of the narrative books. They may be sought in God's injunctions to the Israelites and in the passionate outbursts of the later prophets. One feels them in the soliloquies of the *Psalms* and, in didactic form, in the concise epigrams of the book of *Proverbs*. The emotions of sadness may be expressed in the words of the book of *Lamentations*, and the intimate love conversations arise naturally from the language of the *Song of Songs*. Again a tertiary—or even less direct—source of material for dialogue may be discerned in the natural description embodied in the Bible, which is found in sufficient quantity in the latter *Prophets*, in the *Psalms* and in *Job* to form the basis for the more imaginative and descriptive elements of dialogue.

But in the final analysis the sum total of all the possible materials for dialogue which can be derived from the various strata of the Bible, even by a master of that medium, remains sadly meagre compared to the resources which the novelist, writing in a living idiom, has constantly at his disposal. In *The Love of Zion* the problem is not so acute. The comparative

4. *Job*, i and ii.
5. *I Kings*, iii.

6. See J. Fichman, *Anshei Besorah*, p. 101 f.

brevity of the story, the greater part of which is narrative and descriptive, with the dialogue playing a minor role, alleviates the difficulty; moreover the historical background is, if anything, enhanced by the old-fashioned flavour of the conversation. In some measure, even if to a lesser extent, the same factors mitigate the problem in *The Guilt of Samaria*; although here the greater length and complexity of the novel, with the accompanying greater emphasis on dialogue, tend to make the deficiencies of the medium more obvious. Only the prophetic soliloquies sound a convincing note of truth:

Therefore give ear, rebellious people! Behold your festival has turned to festering, your joy to mourning. The king of Israel is all dark, for Assyria's king has found him false, and cast him in prison. Go to Samaria and see, and know your fate. That is where Beth-El has led you! Thus the fickle prophets have afflicted you! Are you not ashamed of your sacrifices and your Ashtoreths? The king of Assyria has taken the measure of Israel's treachery and renounced his covenant of peace. Now all your eyes are turned to Egypt. But the sky is dark in Tahpanhes also, and your envoys have left king So, in whom you placed your hope, wringing their hands. Ephraim is a crumbling wall, and the storm-wind from the north will send it crashing to eternal ruin. The sanctuaries of Beth-El will fall before its might, and the horns thereof be broken for ever—just as the prophet foretold in Jeroboam's days. Therefore bestir yourselves, O seed of Jacob and remnant of the house of Israel. Unite and band together and return unto the Lord, before your feet stumble on the dark mountains. For the sound of lamentation is heard in Samaria: surely we are ashamed, for our king is taken captive and the princes have lost heart. Repent and call upon your God with all your soul. Perhaps he may yet have mercy on the remnant of Joseph.[7]

But with *The Hypocrite* the limits of Biblical dialogue are

7. *The Guilt of Samaria*, part I, ch. 15.

finally reached. In this novel, which is approximately five times the length of *The Love of Zion* and which depicts the life of his own period, Mapu was compelled to face the inadequacy of his chosen medium. The Biblical flavour of the dialogue is manifestly unsuitable for a novel of contemporary life. A similar phenomenon, indeed, appears in H. Melville's great novel *Moby Dick*, in which some of Captain Ahab's inspired utterances are highly reminiscent of the language of the prophets. But Melville introduces this type of language only sporadically and deliberately, when he feels the medium of contemporary prose inadequate for the emotions to be expressed, while his other characters meanwhile converse in a familiar idiom. Moreover, Biblical terminology is clearly deficient for many of the conversational themes engendered by the problems of modern life which find expression in *The Hypocrite*.[8] In any case Mapu felt himself compelled to break fresh ground and to introduce into his conversation some of the language of later strata of Hebrew literature,[9] and even traces of Aramaic phrases,[10] a device which Mendele Mocher Sefarim (1836–1917) was later to develop so successfully into a comparatively racy and highly colloquial form of dialogue.

It must, then, be conceded *à priori* that the greater part of the dialogue is stilted and artificial, and that despite Mapu's heroic efforts to hammer out his material into pliable form, the direct speech only too frequently lacks vitality. This defect is enhanced by a tendency—found commonly in Biblical Hebrew, and not unknown even in Modern Hebrew—to couch polite conversation in the oblique form. The stilted nature of much of the incidental dialogue may be illustrated from the first meeting of Amnon and Jedidiah, the father of Tamar, whose

8. For detailed information on the nature of the difficulties to be overcome, see D. Patterson 'Some Linguistic Aspects of the Nineteenth-Century Hebrew Novel', in the *Journal of Semitic Studies*, Vol. VII, Autumn, 1962.

9. See above, note 2 to the chapter 'A Neo-Biblical Style', and p. 74, and below, p. 106.

10. Cf. *The Hypocrite*, part II, ch. 12, p. 298; part IV, ch. 1, p. 368.

life has been saved by Amnon's bravery:

> And Jedidiah raised his eyes and said: 'Is your name Amnon?'
>
> And the youth said to him: 'Amnon is the name of your servant.'
>
> 'Are you the one that saved Tamar, my daughter, from the savage lion?'—Jedidiah asked him further.
>
> 'The Lord was pleased to strengthen the hand of your servant'—Amnon answered with modest grace.
>
> 'May the Lord bless you, my son!'—Jedidiah said—'And you will be an honourable man in Zion. Behold! I am in your debt for this deed, and I shall reward you accordingly.'[11]

Not infrequently, however, a more genuine spirit is infused, and the dialogue comes to life. This is especially the case with the villains, who tend to be more convincing than the righteous characters,[12] and whose conversations are often spiced, and on occasion leavened with humour—a quality which the heroes lack entirely! This quality tends to assert itself during bouts of heavy drinking, as when Bukkiah remarks to Carmi, the rascally inn-keeper:

> . . . Now both of us are empty fellows, while our vessels are full of wine. But if the vessels are emptied inside us, we shall become full and the vessels empty. . . .[13]

Of a similar order is Omri's comment when he meets Zimri, his companion in villainy, after a long absence, and attempts to rouse him from sleep with the cutting observation:

> . . . But what are you doing asleep on your feet? Don't you know you've slept right through the end of Ahaz's reign to the beginning of Hezekiah's? . . .[14]

Even more spirited is the lively altercation which takes place

11. *The Love of Zion*, ch. 6, p. 16.
12. See above, p. 60.
13. *The Love of Zion*, ch. 16, p. 42.
14. *The Guilt of Samaria*, part II, ch. 12, p. 171.

between Pethahiah and Jerahmeel, and which, quite apart from the dramatic irony involved, has elements of slapstick humour and colourful phraseology.[15] A similar raciness is found, too, in the preceding passage, in which Pethahiah assures Zadok of his ability to ensure that his rest will not be disturbed,[16] while a brave attempt to portray the language of the street occurs in the lively scene in which Nehemiah's house is picketed.[17] Again a more genuine note is found in the love scenes, where the imaginative language is in keeping with romantic emotions involved, and which nevertheless—as in the reunion of Uzziel and Miriam after many long years of separation—are handled with delicate restraint.[18] In general a gradual maturing of dialogue is observable in the later novels as Mapu acquired more experience in this form of expression; while the longer speeches, which are here much more frequent than in *The Love of Zion*, tend to be more successful than the short, casual snatches of conversation, which, as is well known to students of language, present the greatest idiomatic difficulties.

Closely connected with this latter problem is the manner of introducing direct speech. For the novelist in a modern European language there is a great choice of words for introducing a statement, question or reply, which obviates the monotony of a constantly recurring use of the verbs 'say', 'ask' and 'answer'. In the absence of any such wide range in the Bible, however, Mapu was limited to a very small selection of suitable verbs, a liability which naturally becomes more pronounced where the dialogue consists of brief statement and reply, and the words appear with a proportionate frequency.[19]

15. *The Hypocrite*, part II, ch. 12, p. 299.

16. Ibid., part II, ch. 12, p. 298.

17. Ibid., part IV, ch. 6, p. 381.

18. *The Guilt of Samaria*, part II, ch. 6.

19. The following verbs are used almost exclusively for the introduction of direct speech with the appropriate change of grammatical form as required by gender and number, and the frequent addition of the verbal suffix:

(*a*) The verbs *amar*, *'anah* and *sha'al*. These are in most frequent use.

(*b*) The Biblical form *wa-yo'mer*.

(*c*) The Biblical form *wa-yo'mer el*

The extreme limitation of such verbs and their monotonous
repetition throughout the length of three novels constitute a
serious defect in Mapu's style. They provide one of the most
striking instances of the difficulties involved in the adaptation of
the materials of the Bible to the construction of a modern
novel. For whereas simplicity and repetition of form are
characteristic of the Biblical narrative, and indeed accentuate
its forcefulness and appeal, they are totally unsuited to the
vastly different canvas of the novel, which demands far greater
flexibility and variety. This defect is pathetically obvious and
must be admitted even while recognizing the greatness of
Mapu's feat in creating dialogue and the large measure of
success which he achieved in the attempt. Nevertheless, there
can be little doubt that Mapu's novels, both by virtue of their
own merit, and through the great influence which they exerted
on subsequent Hebrew novelists,[20] helped in no small measure
to prepare the ground for the extraordinary revival of Hebrew
as a spoken language, which Mapu had, himself, so dramatically prophesied.[21]

---

libbo. This is used for soliloquy and
unspoken thought.

(*d*) The verb *dibber* and the
Biblical form *wa-yedabber*, sometimes
followed by the Biblical *le'mor*, and
sometimes by the phrase *et ha-debarim
ha-elleh*.

(*e*) The verbs *kara*, *heri'a* and
hosif which are occasionally introduced for variety.

(*f*) The compound form *'anah
we-amar*, sometimes in the Biblical
form *wa-ya'an wa-yo'mer*.

(*g*) Two rather artificial forms,

which are used—although rarely—
when a contrast of idea between two
persons or two groups of people is
required. In the first case the form is
zeh yo'mar . . . we-re'ehu yashib, and
in the second case *elleh yo'meru. . .
we-elleh ya'anu*.

20. See below, p. 105f.

21. See below, p. 162. For a read-
able description of the revival of
Modern Hebrew as a spoken language, see R. St. John, *Tongue of the
Prophets*, New York, 1952.

GUIDE AND MORALIST

ALTHOUGH in so many respects a revolutionary in the realm of Hebrew literature from the point of view of the form, setting and conception of his novels, Mapu was too much a child of his generation to remain aloof from its missionary spirit. On the contrary he felt himself a conscious champion of the cause of *Haskalah*, and the ideals of that movement, as reflected in the cultural, religious, social and economic struggles of the time, are inextricably embedded in the body of his writings.[1]

The principal ideas, which comprise the element of didacticism in Mapu's novels, and which roughly correspond with the main aims of the movement of *Haskalah*, may be divided into five categories:

1 The glorification of the Jewish past.
2 The encouragement of a discriminating use of the Hebrew language with an attendant refinement of taste.
3 The dissemination of knowledge and enlightenment.
4 The inculcation of a lofty, ethical attitude to life.
5 The improvement of the social and economic position of the Jewish people.

These several aspects, however, are not treated as separate themes, but rather interwoven one with the other to such an extent that the aims appear synonymous and mutually dependent.

The glorification of the Jewish past is, of course, inherent in the very conception of the two historical novels, and embodied in the name *The Love of Zion*. Although couched in very different form these two novels have much in common with the productions of *Hokmat Yisrael*, or *Jewish Science*,[2] which did so much to restore the national pride of the Jewish people. But apart from their historical interest, these stories

1. Cf. P. Laḥower, *Meḥḳarim we-Nisyonot*, p. 45; *Klausner*, p. 343 f.   2. See M. Waxman, op. cit., III, p. 173, and ch. X.

contained a living message for Mapu's own generation. The full, free life of the individual and the national independence, so clearly portrayed in these novels, as well as the healthy and organic connection with the soil, presented such a striking contrast to the harsh reality and meagre existence of contemporary life, that his readers could not but have been awakened to a longing for better things and to the need to break the fetters of gradual decay which enveloped the Jewish community.

It is clearly an exaggeration to portray Mapu as a creator of the Zionist movement,[3] a fact which S. L. Zitron has pointed out.[4] But there can be no doubt that the influence exerted by these novels and the deep longings they aroused helped to prepare a mental climate suitable for the growth of the Zionist idea. It may be doubted whether Mapu's personal conception of a physical return to Palestine went beyond the traditional idea expressed by the ageing Obadiah:

> But be sure of this, that Zion's paths are in my heart, and that as soon as my money is returned, I shall take my staff in my hand and journey to the holy city; for who is there, or what is there, to keep me here?[5]

What is more certain, however, is that his stories represent a symbolic, indeed prophetic, call for national revival,[6] and as such have exercised a profound influence on subsequent generations of young readers.[7]

The same concentration on the land of Israel as the high-water mark in Jewish history and the rallying point for the national pride, which is intrinsic in *The Love of Zion* and *The Guilt of Samaria*, is introduced even into *The Hypocrite*. Azriel's letters from Palestine, which are interspersed throughout this

3. Cf. S. Streit, *Ba-'Alot ha-Shaḥar*, Tel-Aviv, 1927, p. 52.

4. *Yoẓerei ha-Sifrut ha-'Ibrit ha-Ḥadashah*, p. 52.

5. *The Hypocrite*, part V, ch. 5, p. 434.

6. Cf. S. L. Ẓitron, op. cit., p. 52. Also see below, pp. 160 ff.

7. Cf. S. Streit, op. cit., p. 52. See also J. Fichman, *Anshei Besorah*, p. 152. See also D. Patterson, 'Early Zionists and the Great Debate', in *World Jewry*, No. 4, Vol. I, June, 1958. Cf. below, p. 105.

long novel, comprise one of the most attractive and moving elements of the whole work.[8] Mapu was clearly intent on keeping the picture of the land of Israel constantly before his readers. One further note is sounded in *The Guilt of Samaria* which finds its echo in *The Hypocrite*. The conflict of the northern and the southern kingdoms, which forms the historical background of the former novel, and the tragic consequences of disunity for the nation as a whole are continually stressed.[9] The same historical concept is clearly in evidence in the conflict between the Pietists and the *Maskilim*, which forms one of the central themes in *The Hypocrite*. Mapu was anxious to assume the role of mediator between the two extreme parties of his time.[10] In a world of changing values and ideas he constantly strove to keep the balance between the old generation and the new and to foster mutual understanding.[11] Above all things the unity of Israel had to be preserved.

Mapu's love of the Hebrew language was equalled only by his earnest desire to foster its widespread use among his own contemporaries and to raise the aesthetic level of publications in that medium. His motives for writing in Hebrew and his choice of the imaginative story—which he refers to as *Ḥazon* (a vision)—are described in the introduction to the third part of *The Hypocrite*[12] and the introduction to *The Visionaries*.[13] With the publication of his novels in Hebrew, Mapu hoped to attract the young generation to a deeper attachment to that language, and thereby counteract the tendency towards assimilation so conspicuous among the Jewish communities of France and Germany. In addition he believed that by stirring their imagination and widening their mental horizons he would encourage the youth to seek learning and wisdom. Mapu felt deeply the pressing need to raise the general level of taste, and the emphasis on *Ṭub Ṭaʿam* (good taste) is maintained constantly throughout his writings, sometimes under

---

8. See above, p. 36.

9. Cf. *The Guilt of Samaria*, part II, chs. 8 and 18.

10. Cf. J. Fichman, op. cit., p. 118.

11. See the introduction to *The Visionaries, Mapu*, p. 455.

12. Ibid., p. 312. Cf. p. 252.

13. Ibid., p. 457.

the name *Leshon-Limmudim* or *Ẓaḥot* or *Meliẓah*, although the latter term is also used—generally together with the word *Mashal*, as in *Proverbs*, i. 6—in the sense of a penetrating understanding.

One of the clearest examples of this tendency is contained in Ahitub's letter to Naaman in which he describes the virtues of his father Nehemiah, who represents the finest type of *Maskil*, with the words:

> ... He wields no axe or hammer to break down (in the sense of 'expound') the Holy Scriptures, but explains them with judgement and wisely, in terms that are equally comprehensible both to the wise and the unlettered. . . .[14]

On the other hand the orthodox opponents of *Haskalah*, for whom even the study of Hebrew grammar was anathema, are characterized by their utter disregard for the refinements of language as in the case of Hamul:

> And apart from his Talmud, which he had studied since childhood, he knew nothing, but despised *Meliẓah* and *Ẓaḥot* and *Leshon-Limmudim*, which he regarded as vile words and wasted study.[15]

To Mapu fine speech and fine character are almost synonymous and the heroes throughout the novel display a due regard for wisdom and the beauties and subtleties of language. Amnon, for example, is praised with the words:

> For beyond all riches he preferred to understand *Mashal* and *Meliẓah*. . . .[16]

Even the unfortunate Zarah bitterly laments the education which has prevented him from expressing his thoughts delicately:

> ... And to this day I had no one to teach me grammar, due to Gaddiel and Zadok; and even the little I learned in secret,

14. *The Hypocrite*, part I, ch. 5, p. 228.

15. Ibid., part II, ch. 3, p. 263.

16. *The Love of Zion*, ch. 6, p. 18.

I hid away in my heart, without letting it pass my lips, for I sat in my study alone. And so, although I can easily arrange the written word with taste and judgement, I cannot speak a sentence correctly. . . .[17]

The clearest example of Mapu's crusade for the refinement of Hebrew appears, of course, in his own use of the language in his novels, but an additional spur to the development or taste can be felt in the discussions on literature and literary criticism which he portrays inside the framework of *The Hypocrite*.[18]

Closely connected with the call for the refinement of language is Mapu's constant plea for the dissemination of knowledge and enlightenment. Indeed, apart from its intrinsic value, the former concept is regarded as the instrument of the latter. No less than the 'Age of Reason' in France and the 'Enlightenment' in Germany of the previous century, the movement of *Haskalah* believed that the spread of the ideas of reason and understanding would eradicate the evils of society and advance the cause of civilization. In consequence the need for popular enlightenment was regarded as a matter of paramount importance, towards which every effort should be expended. Hence, too, the constant stress on the importance of learning foreign languages—an occupation regarded by the orthodox as anathema. All the virtues required for the new type of being, whose every action would be guided by reason, were embodied in the ideal figure of the *Maskil*. As the spearhead of the attack on the forces of darkness and ignorance, and in spite of all the harm perpetrated by foolishness and superstitious prejudice, the *Maskil* would eventually conquer with the weapons of wisdom, moral superiority and good taste. The concept is stressed continually in Mapu's writings:

Even if fools hide themselves in gloom and desolation, the wise man will gradually lighten our darkness. . . .[19]

17. *The Hypocrite*, part III, ch. 8, p. 342.

18. See especially part V, chs. 3 and 4. Cf. below, p. 163 f.

19. *The Love of Zion*, ch. 10, p. 28.

The bad characters, on the other hand, are conspicuous by their hatred of these qualities:

... But his greatest fault was his complete hatred of knowledge and understanding, of all *Melizah*, *Zaḥot* and *Leshon-Limmudim*. ... [20]

Again in order to worm his way into a position of confidence the villain has only to assume the guise of enlightenment:

And he liked Gaal, because he acted the part of *Maskil* in every particular. ... [21]

Typical of the philosophy Mapu is endeavouring to expound is Amnon's reward for saving Tamar from the lion's jaws. He asks for and is granted an education, while Jedidiah exhorts his instructors:

... Take of your spirit upon him, and give him good counsel, that he may understand *Mashal*, *Melizah* and *Zaḥot*, and know the Lord. [22]

Later, when Amnon becomes a man of war, and turns his attention to the study of military arts, Mapu is still careful to temper the new development with the remark:

... But for all that he never ceased to direct his steps to the gate, to seek God's presence, and in all his ways he was a *Maskil*. [23]

Again in *The Hypocrite* the young Raphael is urged to continue his poetry and studies:

... And in all your ways be a *Maskil*. ... [24]

As a life-long pedagogue, Mapu could not refrain from emphasizing this lesson repeatedly.

One of the keynotes sounded throughout the novels is the

20. *The Hypocrite*, part II, ch. 4, p. 267.
21. Ibid., part I, ch. 2, p. 218.
22. *The Love of Zion*, ch. 6, p. 18.
23. Ibid., ch. 8, p. 23.
24. *The Hypocrite*, part I, ch. 3, p. 223. Cf. *I Samuel*, xviii. 14.

constant stress on a lofty, ethical approach to life, which is again closely associated with refinement of language:

> Behold, *Meliẓah* and morality were twin-born from the beginning of time. . . .[25]

Moral and religious sentiments—modelled on the prophetic books and Wisdom Literature[26] of the Bible, and in the historical novels actually uttered by Biblical prophets[27]—occupy a prominent place in all three stories. They all end happily with a generous reward for the good characters and the shameful exposure and punishment of the villains, who, moreover, regularly repent.[28] In spite of the numerous occasions on which the evil schemes seem certain of victory, in the end truth will out, and no grounds are left for uncertainty that the issue was ever really in doubt. Only too willing to admit his mistake in placing a too naïve trust in men, now unmasked as hypocrites, Jedidiah discerns the hand of God in the final turn of events.[29] His wife Tirzah readily echoes his sentiments:

> But God is good to them that hope for him, and in him we place our trust. . . .[30]

No less expressive of deep faith is Shulamit's cry:

> The Lord sees the tears of every afflicted soul, and my tears too, and he will heal the broken-hearted, and redeem the captives of war.[31]

Again the two villains Hepher and Bukkiah are described as having lost God's grace on the day of their crimes, and never prospering subsequently.[32] Even if, at times, a suggestion of

25. Ibid., part I, ch. 5, p. 228.

26. The Wisdom Literature of the Bible was frequently echoed by the exponents of *Haskalah*. Cf. M. Waxman, op cit., III, pp. 122 ff.

27. See above, p. 59.

28. See above, p. 57.

29. *The Love of Zion*, ch. 24, p. 58.

30. Ibid., ch. 27, p. 63.

31. *The Guilt of Samaria*, part I, ch. 5, p. 93.

32. *The Love of Zion*, ch. 8, p. 21.

the problem of the book of *Job* emerges as in the outburst:

O righteous God! Why do the violent flourish?[33]

in the end poetic justice prevails.

Throughout the novels a constant barrage is directed against fraud, deceit and especially hypocrisy, which is made the central target for Mapu's scorn, and which in *The Hypocrite* is treated as a principal theme, incorporated in the very title. In this novel it is closely associated with forgery, also an integral element in the plot. It is of interest, however, that neither the frequent interception of letters, nor the constant reading of correspondence addressed to other persons, nor the practice of listening to a conversation behind closed doors[34] is censured despite their contravention of Jewish ethics.[35] This fact constitutes a further illustration of the dubious morality even of some of the good characters, which has been pointed out,[36] and hardly accords with the stress Mapu lays on the importance of good deeds as well as piety:

> And yet I have known men who occupy themselves with ethics all day, and from too much contemplation of ethics they do not see their fellow-men for looking at the heavens. . . .[37]

Mapu does, however, realize the dilemma of the intelligent, when confronted with seeming inconsistencies between reason and faith, and attempts to point a solution in the person of Nehemiah, the true *Maskil*.[38]

One further ethical standpoint is worthy of note. Throughout the novels the concept of faithful and devoted love is put forward as the perfect relationship between man and woman,

33. *The Guilt of Samaria*, part I, ch. 7, p. 100.

34. *The Hypocrite*, part III, ch. 9, p. 347.

35. See, e.g., H. Graetz, *Geschichte der Juden*, Leipzig, 1895, Vol. V, p. 336 f.

36. *Klausner*, p. 340. See also A. Sha'anan, '*Iyyunim be-Sifrut ha-Haskalah*, p. 164 f. Cf. above, p. 58.

37. *The Hypocrite*, part II, ch. 3, p. 265.

38. Ibid., part IV, ch. 14, p. 404.

as illustrated by Tirzah's remark:

> A man can do no better than to take one wife, and go through life loving her.[39]

If this does not always accord with the practice of the Biblical story, it appears, nevertheless, to have been a fundamental tenet in Mapu's own ethical conceptions.[40]

Wretchedly poor all his life and himself a victim of the crushing poverty in which the Jews of eastern Europe lived, Mapu could hardly refrain from suggesting improvements in the social and economic conditions of his people. In the historical novels he portrays the varied pursuits of the individuals of an independent nation, with due emphasis on the agricultural backbone of the economy, and the satisfaction to be derived from such a livelihood.[41] In *The Hypocrite* he develops the theme further. A part of the practical work undertaken by the *Maskilim* consisted of attempts to found societies for the promotion of agriculture among the Jews[42] which, it was supposed, would provide a healthy and constructive solution to the unbalanced Jewish economy. In his novel of contemporary life Mapu heartily takes up the cause, and champions a 'Back to the Land' campaign,[43] suitably endowing his young hero Naaman with the profession of agricultural scientist.

Frequently, too, the story serves as a forum for his ideas on education, wherein he forcefully portrays the bad effects of harsh and exclusive book-learning,[44] so widely practised by the Pietists, and advocates his own use of more gentle methods.[45] The barbaric practice of burning secular books is censured severely,[46] while the underhand methods of the traditional 'match-maker', quite indifferent to the happiness of the young

39. *The Love of Zion*, ch. 2, p. 6.

40. In *The Guilt of Samaria*, however, Miriam allows the unhappy Jehosheba to become a second wife to her husband. See above, p. 61.

41. *The Love of Zion*, ch. 7, p. 19. Cf. above, pp. 45 f. and 55.

42. J. S. Raisin, *The Haskalah Movement in Russia*, Philadelphia, 1913, pp. 140–4.

43. *The Hypocrite*, part I, ch. 7, p. 233. See also part I, ch. 14, p. 253; part V, ch. 7, p. 440.

44. Ibid., part I, ch. 5, p. 226.

45. Ibid., part II, ch. 3, p. 266.

46. Ibid.

couples whose marriages he is so anxious to arrange, receive a due share of satire![47] A further reform, strongly advocated, is the emancipation of woman. Elisheba is the representative of the new type of woman, independent, cultured, demanding equality of education with her male counterpart.[48] It is significant, too, that Mapu stresses her interest in handicrafts as a field of creative and aesthetic expression.[49] His advocacy of economic and social reform, however, is generally moderate and restrained in comparison to the bitter polemics which abound in the novels of his successors, who frequently resort to cutting satire and biting irony for the propagation of their views.[50]

But the solutions put forward for the social and economic evils of Jewish life are sketchy and inadequate. It is, indeed, doubtful whether the problems involved were deeply understood. There are, at least, indications that Mapu did not always feel sure of his ground. In *The Hypocrite* he portrayed a negative type of *Maskil* in the person of Emil,[51] who represents the type of young man completely estranged from his people. But Mapu also criticizes severely the so-called 'Maskilim', whose claims to literary ability are quite unfounded.[52] In the introduction to the third part of *The Hypocrite* he bitterly laments the fact that the new generation is no longer interested in Hebrew literature; and perhaps there is more than an historical echo in the warning that Uzziel gives of the uselessness of preaching in Ephraim.[53] But for the most part Mapu points his lesson in good faith, on the one hand fighting to preserve the finer elements of Jewish tradition, and on the other indicating the new values to be adopted in a changing world.

47. Ibid., part I, ch. 9.

48. Ibid., part I, ch. 12, p. 247. Cf. above, pp. 52 and 61.

49. *The Hypocrite*, part III, ch. 11, p. 353. Cf. R. A. Braudes, *Ha-Dat we-ha-Ḥayyim*, Lemberg, 1885, pt. 2, pp. 12 and 189.

50. Cf. below, p. 105 f.

51. See J. Klausner, *Yoẓerim u-Bonim*, p. 188.

52. *The Hypocrite*, part II, ch. 3, p. 266.

53. *The Guilt of Samaria*, part II, ch. 8, p. 159.

MAPU'S CONTRIBUTION TO HEBREW LITERATURE

An evaluation of Mapu's contribution to Hebrew literature involves some consideration of his own debt to previous writers both in Hebrew and in European languages.[1] His celebrity is firmly based on precedence. He was the first to create a Hebrew novel, and thereby paved the way for the emergence of this important branch of modern Hebrew literature. But many of the component features of his novels, and particularly the mechanics of his plots, were derived from a number of sources. Mapu's originality lay in the overall conception of his works, and in the skilful adaptation of his material. That his inventive capacity was limited is demonstrated both by his frequent borrowing of dramatic devices and by the many repetitions and similarities which occur throughout his novels.[2]

The influence of the Bible on Mapu's works is most conspicuous in the setting, style and language of the historical novels, and extends in less measure to *The Hypocrite*. It constitutes the primary source of Mapu's inspiration. Due regard, however, must be given to the importance of the Hebrew poets Moses Ḥayyim Luzzatto and Naphtali Herz Wessely (1725–1805), both of whom Mapu held in high esteem.[3] The influence of the latter is less specific, being apparent in tendencies rather than in detail, and stems principally from his magnum opus *Shirei-Tif'eret*.[4] This work comprises a long epic poem, dealing with Moses and the Exodus from Egypt, and modelled on the *Messias* of the German poet G. F. Klopstock (1724–1803). Although the poem is no longer rated very highly, it was loudly acclaimed by the poet's own generation,

---

1. For his knowledge of the languages see above, p. 16.

2. See above, p. 33 f.

3. Cf. the significant reference to M. H. Luzzatto's drama *La-Yesharim*

Tehillah and N. H. Wessely's poem *Shirei-Tif'eret* in *The Hypocrite*, part II, ch. 7, p. 282.

4. See M. Waxman, op. cit., III, pp. 108 ff.

and Wessely was considered for a time the leading poet of the day.[5]

Wessely introduced new forms into Hebrew poetry which were followed by Hebrew poets for more than sixty years,[6] and which may be discerned in the songs interspersed by Mapu in his own novels.[7] Mapu, however, displayed little poetic inspiration. His poems are clumsy and wooden, written in a halting rhythm, and with a scansion often imperfect. They represent one of the least convincing elements of his stories, and provide an interesting example of a literary climate which fostered the composition of Hebrew poetry almost as a duty regardless of any lack of poetic talent on the part of the writer.[8] Moreover, the poems in the historical novels are quite anachronistic in form.[9] Their European metre and rhyme are quite foreign to the poetry of the Bible.[10] In this respect Mapu was, perhaps, influenced by Bulwer Lytton's *The Last Days of Pompeii*, in which many songs in European form are introduced anachronistically into an historical framework, and with which Mapu may have been familiar in its German or French translation.[11] In any case the phenomenon of 'Biblical' songs in modern rhythm was sufficiently common in Hebrew drama to be acceptable, while a fondness for lyric poetry, particularly that of the French, German and English romantic movements in literature, is evident in the second period of *Haskalah*—a tendency best exemplified by Mapu's contemporary,

---

5. Ibid.

6. The favourite stanza contains six lines with a rhyme scheme a.a.b.c.c.b. See ibid., p. 114.

7. There are eight songs in *The Love of Zion*, five in *The Guilt of Samaria* and two in *The Hypocrite*. See D. Patterson, 'The Use of Songs in the Novels of Abraham Mapu', in the *Journal of Semitic Studies*, Vol. I, No. 4, October, 1956.

8. Cf. D. Patterson, *The Founda-*

tions of Modern Hebrew Literature, London, 1961, pp. 41 ff.

9. Cf. J. Klausner, *Yoẓerim u-Bonim*, p. 179; also *Klausner*, p. 292.

10. Cf. G. B. Gray, *The Forms of Hebrew Poetry*, London, 1915.

11. Cf. *Klausner*, p. 292. In the English novel, however, the songs represent a far more integral element, and despite the modern rhyme and metre are much more akin to the classical spirit.

Micah Joseph Lebensohn (1825-52).[12] But an experiment of this nature can prove successful only in the hands of a genuine poet, and Mapu's complete lack of self-criticism with regard to his poetic compositions sadly undermines the effect.

Wessely's influence on the novelist, however, consists of idea rather than form. The poem *Shirei-Tif'eret* focused attention upon the Bible as source material for modern literary composition. By utilizing the events narrated in the book of *Exodus* as the basis for an epic poem, Wessely demonstrated the inherent possibilities of the Bible. Moreover, he helped to revive the Biblical style in Hebrew literature by his attempt to mould the language into a form sufficiently pliable for the needs of a large-scale epic. The linguistic problems confronting him in this task were not unlike those which Mapu had to face in the adaptation of the language of the Bible for a modern novel. There can be little doubt that Mapu paid careful attention to Wessely's achievement, while evaluating his own chances of success in the utilization both of a Biblical setting and of Biblical language as the twin foundations of his historical novels.

But the influence of Wessely stems also from another source. The poet was a champion of the movement of enlightenment. A series of letters addressed to various Jewish communities was later collected in book form under the title *Diberei-Shalom we-Emet*.[13] In these letters Wessely advocated reforms in the Jewish educational system calculated to widen its scope and introduce secular knowledge. In regarding the expansion of the Jewish curriculum of studies as a prime essential for the amelioration of the social and economic position of the Jews, Wessely helped to establish the principles of *Haskalah*, and his ideas are echoed in Mapu's novels, particularly *The Hypocrite*.

The influence of Moses Hayyim Luzzatto is more direct,[14]

---

12. For an interesting illustration of M. J. Lebensohn's translation from Lamartine, see K. A. Bertini's article in *Gilyonot*, Tel-Aviv, 1952, Vol. 27, No. 7, p. 9.

13. See M. Waxman, op. cit., III, pp. 114 ff.

14. See P. Laḥower, *Meḥḳarim we-Nisyonot*, p. 50, esp. footnote; also J. Fichman, *Anshei Besorah*, p. 83.

and traces of it are discernible in the plots, dramatic devices, background and ideas common to both authors. The process is most in evidence in *The Love of Zion*, in which novel elements from Luzzatto's allegorical dramas *Migdal 'Oz* and *La-Yesharim Tehillah* have been freely adopted.[15] From the latter Mapu utilized the device of the betrothal of babies. In *La-Yesharim Tehillah* Yosher the son of Emet is pledged to Tehillah the daughter of Hamon. In *The Love of Zion* Joram and Jedidiah make an even more premature covenant, and pledge their children before birth. Again the exchange of Nabal for Azrikam, which is one of the determining factors of the plot of *The Love of Zion*, is paralleled by the exchange of Rahab for Yosher, upon which the whole story of *La-Yesharim Tehillah* is built. Moreover the dream of Hananeel, which plays an important part in the novel, is modelled on the dream of King Ram in *Migdal 'Oz*.

In addition to these major similarities of plot, Mapu made use of Luzzatto's minor dramatic devices. Adah's plot[16] to incriminate Shelomith by sending a poisoned gift to Ziphah is reminiscent of Zimri's villainy in putting poison in the wine sent by Amnon to Tamar.[17] Again the false accusation brought against Shelomith[18] parallels that levelled at Naame and Shoshanah.[19] The influence of the allegorical dramas extends even to *The Hypocrite*. The violent storm which is appeased only by the deaths of the wicked Zaphnath and Emil[20] echoes the storm which serves as a *deus ex machina* in *La-Yesharim Tehillah*, and results in the unmasking of Rahab and Tarmit.[21]

J. Klausner, however, denies the influence of M. H. Luzzatto on Mapu, *Klausner*, p. 336. For Luzzatto's influence on subsequent Hebrew drama see D. Patterson, 'Hebrew Drama', in the *Bulletin of the John Rylands Library*, Vol. 43, No. 1, September, 1960, pp. 98 ff.

15. For a summary of the plots of these dramas see S. Ginsburg, *The Life and Works of Moses Hayyim Luzzatto*, pp. 104 ff.

16. *Migdal 'Oz*, III, 2.
17. *The Love of Zion*, ch. 21.
18. *Migdal 'Oz*, IV, 2.
19. *The Love of Zion*, ch. 24.
20. *The Hypocrite*, part IV, ch. 17.
21. Act III, scene 1.

A further point of similarity lies in the idyllic setting of Luzzatto's dramas[22] and the idyllic element which occurs in Mapu's novels, particularly *The Love of Zion*.[23] Both authors stress the superiority of the simple, rustic life and the homely pleasures of the shepherd, which compare so favourably with the restless dissatisfaction of the city-dweller.[24] Both authors frequently resort to the device of soliloquy for the expression of their ideas.[25] There is a marked similarity between Tehillah pouring out her sorrow in the field[26] and Amnon bitterly lamenting at the water's edge.[27] Again both Luzzatto and Mapu portray simple but romantic love which triumphs over every obstacle for its fulfilment, and which completely dominates the lives of the central characters.

A common feature of both the dramas and the novels is the naïveté of the characters, who merely symbolize virtue and vice, and who, in *La-Yesharim Tehillah*, frankly bear names representative of their specific attributes.[28] The allegorical nature of Luzzatto's work appears in Mapu's novels in the triumph of good over evil, and reason over stupidity. Both writers display marked didactic tendencies and are characterized by their lofty ethical teachings. Both exhibit a deep interest in nature, unusual among Hebrew writers even in Mapu's days: and there is a strong resemblance between Meḥḳar's well-known speech in praise of nature[29] and Amnon's words:

> Thus even the plants of the field can teach us, and from whatever our eyes behold we can draw a moral. . . .[30]

Finally the lucid Hebrew, which Luzzatto employs with

22. *Migdal 'Oz* closely follows the well-known pastoral drama *Il Pastor Fido* by Giovanni Battista Guarini (1537–1612). Cf. S. Ginsburg, op. cit., pp. 96 ff.

23. See above, pp. 45 ff.

24. Cf. *La-Yesharim Tehillah*, I, 3; *Migdal 'Oz*, III, 1; *The Love of Zion*, ch. 7; *The Hypocrite*, part V, ch. 7.

25. See above, p. 45 f. Also *La-Yesharim Tehillah*, I, 1 and 4; II, 1 and 2; *Migdal 'Oz*, I, 2 and 4; III, 1 and 2; IV, 2 and 4.

26. *La-Yesharim Tehillah*, II, 3.

27. *The Love of Zion*, ch. 23.

28. See above, p. 53 f.

29. *La-Yesharim Tehillah*, II, 2.

30. *The Love of Zion*, ch. 4.

such skill and dexterity, and which infuses a spirit of freshness and life into the dramas, is reminiscent of Mapu's own lyrical prose. It would seem that a strong tie of sympathy existed between the minds of the mystic, Luzzatto, and the romantic dreamer, Mapu.

There is reason to believe that Mapu may also have been influenced by a group of Hebrew dramatists writing in Germany in the early nineteenth century. Although almost all these writers have vanished into oblivion, Professor Rabin has demonstrated the part they once played in the literature of the *Haskalah*.[31] Apart from an interesting attempt by I. B. Bing of Würzburg to create a Hebrew slang, a number of other writers connected with Breslau composed several romantic plays on Biblical and post-Biblical themes, apparently inspired directly or indirectly by Joseph Ephrati, the author of a popular drama devoted to the reign of King Saul entitled *Melukat Sha'ul* (Vienna, 1794). Their foremost representative, David Zamoscz, composed, apart from a Biblical drama, two realistic plays devoted to the problems of contemporary German-Jewish society. As social themes were destined to become predominant in Hebrew literature from the sixties of the nineteenth century onwards, Zamoscz may be regarded as something of a pioneer. These playwrights may well have influenced Mapu not only in his historical novels—the drinking scenes in Carmi's inn provide, perhaps, a case in point—but also in his social novel, which played so important a role in directing the attention of modern Hebrew literature towards the compelling problems of contemporary Jewish life.

Among the writers of Hebrew prose whose influence may be discerned in Mapu's novels, due regard should be paid to Joseph Perl and Isaac Erter.[32] As exponents of *Haskalah* in Galicia, these writers poured forth their satires against the social evils of their time in quasi-novel form. Mapu was able to profit by their example in the technique of story-telling, and

31. See C. Rabin, ''Olelot le-Toledot ha-Dramah ba-Haskalah ha-Germanit', in *Melilah*, Vol. 5, 1955; also D. Patterson, 'Hebrew Drama', op. cit., p. 102, n. 1.

32. See above, p. 55.

they provided a precedent for the melodramatic and far-fetched incidents to which Mapu was so prone.[33] Moreover he was quick to incorporate two further characteristics of these writers. Perl and Erter made constant use of letters and dreams as suitable media for their barbs of satire. These methods seemed to clothe their ideas with a certain objectivity, allowing the authors greater freedom of expression. Both these phenomena appear frequently in Mapu's novels.[34] Again the didactic element in Mapu's writings owes much to Perl and Erter.[35] Although Mapu's polemicism is far less vituperative and his approach much more cautious[36] than the stinging attacks of his older contemporaries, he was nevertheless no less anxious to alter the superstitions, narrow educational methods and spiritual poverty of his brethren. Like them he felt that the solution to the economic plight of Russian Jewry lay in agricultural settlement, and he incorporated his ideas in the person of Naaman, the young hero of *The Hypocrite*.[37]

Turning to writers in European languages, Mapu seems to have been influenced principally by the French romantic novelists, the elder Dumas and Eugène Sue.[38] The notion originated from a letter received by R. Brainin from Dr L. Mapu, the author's son, stating that his father was influenced by the French romantic writers, particularly Victor Hugo, Dumas-Père and Eugène Sue.[39] Moreover Brainin asserts, on the authority of D. Z. Bramson, a close acquaintance of Mapu's youth, that the latter considered Sue to be the foremost exponent of the art of the novel.[40] It is true that Mapu strongly opposed the translation of Sue's novels into Hebrew.[41] But

33. See above, pp. 32 ff.

34. See above, pp. 35 f. and 55 f.

35. See above, p. 54.

36. See above, p. 88.

37. See above, p. 94.

38. This idea is developed by J. Klausner, *Klausner*, pp. 289 ff., and especially A. Sha'anan, '*Iyyunim be-Sifrut ha-Haskalah*, part III, chs. 3 and

4. S. L. Zitron, however, minimizes this influence, *Yozerei ha-Sifrut ha-'Ibrit ha-Hadashah*, p. 69.

39. R. Brainin, *Abraham Mapu*, p. 49.

40. Ibid.

41. See Mapu's letters edited by M. Dolitsky, *Shebet Sofer*, Vienna, 1883, p. 125 f. Eugène Sue's novel *Mystères de Paris*, 1842, was translated

מִסְתְּרֵי פַּארִיז

היא הַמַחברת המהֻללה אשר חֻבְּרה בלשון צרפת בִּיד אַבִּיר
הסופרים אייזען סֶי , ונעתקה לכל הלשונות המְתהלכות
בארץ , ועתה גם לשְפת עֵבֶר צָחָה וברורה , בִּיד

קלמן שולמאן

חלק ראשון

— ◦ —

ווילנא

בדפוס ר' יוסף ראובן בר' מנחם מן ראם

שנת תרי"ז לפ"ק

МИСТРЭ ПАРИЗЪ,
т. е.
Тайны Парижскія
Переведенныя на чисто-библейскій языкъ К. Шульманомъ.
часть I.

ВИЛЬНО.
въ Типографіи Р. М. Ромма
1857.

Title-page of the first volume of Kalman Schulman's Hebrew
translation of Eugène Sue's *Mystères de Paris.*—See pp.102ff.

the reason may well be, as A. Sha'anan suggests,[42] that this antagonism stemmed from Mapu's knowledge that his own novel, *The Love of Zion*, owed much to Sue's *Mystères de Paris*, whose publication lowered the value of the originality of his novel in his own eyes. Certainly Mapu experienced pangs of jealousy at the immediate success of K. Schulman's translation, and the financial gain which the translator enjoyed.[43]

Whereas the influence of Victor Hugo on Mapu's novels seems very doubtful,[44] traces of the stamp of both Dumas-Père and Eugène Sue are discernible in Mapu's creations.[45] From the former may be traced the portrayal of the national past.[46] Like Dumas-Père, Mapu chose love and heroism as the dominant factors of his historical novels, especially *The Love of Zion*. In *The Guilt of Samaria* he followed the French novelist in setting his fiction in an historical framework without destroying it. Like his predecessor Mapu mingled historical personages with his own creations.[47] The fusion of exciting adventures, heroic deeds, passionate loves and state intrigues, which comprise the plot of *Les Trois Mousquetaires*,[48] is not less marked in *The Guilt of Samaria*. Moreover, the idealization of Mapu's young heroines[49] is once more reminiscent of the French writer. The influence of Dumas-Père is largely external. From him Mapu learned the art of creating atmosphere, and of clothing his plots in a romantic-historical mantle.

The influence of Eugène Sue, on the other hand, is more

---

into Hebrew during the years 1857–60 by Kalman Schulman.

42. *'Iyyunim be-Sifrut ha-Haskalah*, p. 145.

43. See Mapu's letter quoted in *Klausner*, p. 289 f.

44. J. Klausner rightly points out that Hugo's strong sense of pathos is almost entirely lacking in Mapu's novels, *Klausner*, p. 289. See above, p. 62, however, for remarks on the character of Ezra in *The Hypocrite*. A. Sha'anan also admits inability to

trace any influence of Hugo on Mapu, op. cit., p. 149.

45. See A. Sha'anan, op. cit., pp. 141–67, passim.

46. This aspect may be traced back via Dumas-Père to Walter Scott. However, the influence of Shneur Sachs must also be remembered in this respect. See above, p. 18.

47. See above, p. 59.

48. Paris, 1844.

49. See above, p. 60 f.

clearly discernible in the aim of Mapu's novels, particularly that of *The Hypocrite*. The *Mystères de Paris* was primarily considered a militant social novel,[50] and in common with *The Hypocrite* it presents a social purpose within a romantic setting. Both novels aim to portray existing social evils, and suggest reform. But whereas Sue depicts an economic struggle between the upper and lower strata of Paris society, Mapu outlines an ideological conflict between the old and new generations inside the Jewish community. A further similarity between *Mystères de Paris* and *The Hypocrite* lies in the complexities of the plots, which abound with melodrama, conspiracy and timely coincidence. The villainies perpetrated in *The Hypocrite* are reminiscent of those committed in the underworld of Paris. The villains themselves possess a quality of realism[51] unusual in Mapu's characters but typical of Sue, while both authors display a fondness for idealized heroes and heroines. The mixture of romanticism and realism which pervades Mapu's novel of contemporary life may well have been derived from the French novelist. But while the violence and intrigue encountered in the French novel are perfectly in keeping with the Paris underworld which the story depicts, the attempt to superimpose such elements upon the background of Jewish society in Eastern Europe, which was characterized by sobriety, timidity and a rigid control of the passionate emotions, is primarily responsible for the incongruity of the setting and the plot.

In the light of the various factors outlined above, it may be seen that Mapu's creative power must not be sought in the form of his novels. The structure, the dramatic technique and the characterizations all lean heavily on previous writers, and all display grave weaknesses and limitations. From a technical standpoint Mapu resembles a clumsy apprentice rather than a finished craftsman. He never mastered the art of weaving a convincing plot, and his inability to sustain interest over long periods is particularly evident in his more lengthy novels.[52]

50. See, e.g., Karl Marx's essay on the *Mystères* in *German Ideology* (1846).

51. See above, p. 60.

52. See above, p. 30 f.

Nevertheless, Mapu's writings are stamped with a freshness and originality which more than atone for all his borrowings and limitations, and display an element of genius.

Mapu's main contribution to Hebrew literature appears in the overall conception of his works. He possessed an imagination and descriptive power that could bring dry bones to life. In his historical novels he made the Bible live and endowed a remote period in history with a vividness and freshness of appeal such as no commentary or explanation can offer. His greatness consisted not so much in the intrinsic value of his writings as in the possibilities that he revealed, which placed him at the head of a new literary epoch. His strength lay in the portrayal of setting, in the smoothness of his style, in his mastery of Biblical language. He clearly indicated that the Hebrew language might eventually be forged into an adequate medium of expression and adapted to serve the manifold needs of modern life. And above all he gave vent to the free expression of emotion, transfusing a somewhat dry and intellectual literature with the feelings of heroism and love.[53] His novels provided an emotional stimulus to generations of young readers,[54] fostering a pride in the national past and focusing attention upon the Holy Land. Hence, their influence on the Jewish national movement from which Zionism later emerged constitutes an important factor in modern Jewish history.

His importance is almost equally in evidence in another direction. The ideas on social and educational reform,

53. Cf. above, p. 28 f., and see especially the remarks of P. Smolenskin in *Ha-To'eh be-Darekei ha-Hayyim*, part I, pp. 162 ff. Mapu's influence is also evident in the writings of many minor novelists whose works are now virtually forgotten, e.g. J. Leinwand, '*Oseh Mezimmot*, Lemberg, part I, 1875, part 2, 1876; S. F. Meinkin, *Ahabat Yesharim*, part I, Vilna, 1881; B. I. Zobeizensky, *Ahabat Zaddikim*, Warsaw, 1881; N. M. Sheikewitz, *Ha-Niddahat*, parts I and II, Vilna, 1886, part III, Warsaw, 1887 (see part I, p. 8, footnote). For the influence of Mapu on Israel Weisbrem see D. Patterson, 'Israel Weisbrem: A Forgotten Hebrew Novelist of the Nineteenth Century', in the *Journal of Semitic Studies*, Vol. 4, No. 1, January, 1959, p. 44, n. 1, p. 45, n. 7. Mapu's novels are satirized, however, by A. S. Rabinowitz in '*Al ha-Perek*, Warsaw, 1887, pp. 51 and 86.

54. See above, p. 87.

expounded in *The Hypocrite*, helped to set a fashion among the Hebrew writers who followed him. The influence of the elements of realism in his novel of contemporary life may be traced in the writings of P. Smolenskin (1842–85), J. L. Gordon, R. A. Braudes (1851–1902), M. D. Brandstätter (1844–1928) and Mendele Mocher Sefarim, who developed the positivist and social aspects of their work still further.[55] Indeed, the realist novel depicting the problems of contemporary society has continued to occupy the dominant position in Hebrew literature to the present day. It is of interest, however, that none of the major novelists who succeeded Mapu attempted to imitate his strict Biblical style. Little by little they began to follow Mapu's own advice in utilizing the linguistic resources of later strata of Hebrew literature.[56] Either they lacked Mapu's facility and mastery of the language of the Bible, or they felt that his three novels had exhausted the possibilities of that medium, and sought a richer and more flexible instrument of language. But in any case, the clumsiness of Biblical Hebrew as a means of depicting the complex phenomena of the modern world became increasingly apparent as the range of subject-matter depicted in the Hebrew novel widened.[57]

Of the three novels *The Love of Zion* remains the most significant. It was this first novel that really broke fresh ground, that opened up the prospect of a free and independent life to a people hopelessly cramped and fettered by political, social and economic restrictions. For Mapu's contemporary public *The Love of Zion* depicted a new world. This achievement, as a pointer to Mapu's contribution as a novelist, deserves serious attention. As F. R. Leavis has remarked:

> . . . it is well to start by distinguishing the few really great—the major novelists who count in the same way as the major poets, in the sense that they not only change the

---

55. Cf. above, p. 94 f.

56. See above, note 2 to the chapter 'A Neo-Biblical Style', and pp. 74f. and 82.

57. See D. Patterson, *The Hebrew Novel in Czarist Russia*, Edinburgh University Press, 1964.

possibilities of the art for practitioners and readers, but that they are significant in terms of the human awareness they promote; awareness of the possibilities of life.[58]

If this criterion has real validity, then *The Love of Zion* must bear the stamp of greatness. For not only did it create—not merely change—the possibilities for a Hebrew novel, but in addition it gave open expression to the mute longings and half-sensed gropings of a whole people towards a fuller and richer life.

58. *The Great Tradition*, 1948, p. 2.

PART TWO

In the following translations an attempt has been made to preserve something of the flavour of Abraham Mapu's style. Although not always literal they follow the originals closely, deviating only in accordance with the demands of English idiom. In this way it is hoped that the selected passages may serve to illustrate some of the major features of the novelist's imaginative power. It may be readily conceded that many of the qualities of the original defy adequate translation.

THE PLOT OF 'THE LOVE OF ZION'

Two nobly born and wealthy friends, Joram, an officer in the army, and Jedidiah, a minister of the royal treasury, live in Jerusalem during the reign of King Ahaz. Joram has two wives, Haggith and Naame, of whom Naame, although barren, is the favourite. Finally, however, she conceives, and before going to war against the Philistines Joram entrusts his family to Jedidiah's care, making a covenant with him that in the event of Naame bearing a son and Jedidiah's wife, Tirzah, a daughter, the children shall be betrothed. Meanwhile his other wife, Haggith, bears a son, Azrikam, and employs as nurse her servant Helah, who has also given birth to a son, Nabal.

After Joram's capture, Haggith becomes mistress of the household, treating the servants cruelly. As a result Akan, Helah's husband, complains of her to Mattan, one of the judges of Jerusalem. Mattan, a rejected suitor of Haggith, persuades Akan to set fire to the house, burn Haggith and her children, substitute his own son Nabal for Azrikam and put the blame on Naame. In consequence Naame is forced to flee to Abishai, one of Joram's shepherds near Bethlehem, who sends her to Sitri on the Carmel. There Naame gives birth to a twin son and daughter, Amnon and Peninah. Her guilt is subsequently confirmed in court on the testimony of false witnesses, instigated by Mattan. Jedidiah, however, remains faithful to his word, and manages Joram's estates, bringing up the supposed son of Joram together with his own son Teman, and his daughter Tamar.

About this time the northern kingdom of Samaria falls, and Jedidiah's father-in-law Hananeel is among the captives. Zimri, a priest of Baal, escapes from the captivity, bringing a letter from Hananeel which describes a dream according to which a young man, claiming to be the lover of his granddaughter Tamar, promises to rescue him. Hananeel has also given Zimri his seal, which the latter keeps for future use. Tirzah is deeply influenced by the letter, while Jedidiah makes the villainous Zimri manager of his estate.

In the course of time Tamar grows into a lovely maiden, but Azrikam develops into an ugly and unpleasant youth, despised both by Tamar and by her brother Teman. Their constant disputes induce Jedidiah to settle Azrikam on his 'father's' estates. One day Tamar is attacked by a lion near Bethlehem, and rescued by a handsome shepherd who wins her heart. This shepherd is Amnon, who has grown up in ignorance of his noble birth, and is therefore afraid to return Tamar's love. He accepts, however, her invitation to celebrate the Feast of Weeks at her father's house in Jerusalem.

Meanwhile Teman, on a visit to Joram's estates on the Carmel, chances upon a lovely girl—in reality Peninah, Amnon's sister—who thinks her mother to be a Philistine woman. Teman falls in love with her, but having agreed to wait for three days for an answer finds that at the end of that time both she and her mother have departed without trace, leaving Teman bitterly disappointed.

At the Feast of Weeks Amnon comes to Jedidiah's house in Jerusalem, is received most cordially and accepts an invitation to remain, becoming successively a disciple of the prophets and a member of the royal cavalry. The growing intimacy between Amnon and Tamar, however, is distasteful to Azrikam, who seeks the advice of the crafty Zimri. The latter forges a message from Hananeel, using his seal for the purpose, wherein he relates that he is dying and sends his blessing to Tirzah. Jedidiah credulously believes in the trustworthiness of the message, and loses faith in Hananeel's dream with its description of a youth resembling Amnon. Tirzah and Tamar, on the other hand, continue to believe in the dream. Zimri, therefore, informs Jedidiah of the love which his daughter has conceived for Amnon. Anxious to keep his covenant with Joram, Jedidiah sends Amnon from his house.

Mattan, in the meantime, suffers pangs of remorse and sends for Jedidiah to confess his crime. But death anticipates the disclosure, and he is able only to turn over the key to his treasure-house. Jedidiah is astonished to find it full of Joram's treasures, and entrusts them to the court. In a similar mood of remorse

Akan informs Amnon that Hananeel is still alive and advises him to attempt his rescue. Akan plans to marry his own son Azrikam to Peninah, Amnon's sister. Amnon follows his advice, goes to Assyria and brings back Hananeel. In the ensuing jubilation even Jedidiah has to consent to the marriage of his daughter to Amnon. The arch-villain Zimri, however, plays a trump card. Having spied on Amnon for months, he has seen him visit his mother and sister in their hiding place. He jumps to the conclusion that Amnon is in love with the girl, and informs Tamar, who shows Amnon her displeasure. In despair Amnon asks Zimri for advice! At his suggestion he sends Tamar a letter begging for forgiveness together with a bottle of wine. Zimri first puts poison in the wine, and then informs Tamar of Amnon's treachery. His guilt thus proven, Tamar bids Amnon leave Jerusalem, and he joins the expedition against the Philistines.

Zimri completes his villainy by accusing Amnon's mother and sister of sorcery. But Akan is overcome with remorse and confesses his sin to Azrikam, revealing himself to be the latter's father. To silence him Azrikam sets fire to his house, and stabs his mother. Brought to court with the dying Akan, the machinations are revealed, and the exonerated Naame and Peninah are returned to their inheritance.

Jerusalem, meanwhile, is thrown into confusion by the approach of Sennacherib. This anxiety is heightened in Jedidiah's household by the rumour that Amnon has been taken captive by the Philistines and sold as a slave on the island of Crete. The city, however, is miraculously saved from the invader, and the news of the deliverance spreads throughout the surrounding peoples. As a result Amnon and an old man, who has befriended him, are released and return to Jerusalem. The old man turns out to be Joram, and both families are joyfully reunited.

THE LOVE OF ZION

CHAPTER 4

WITH the coming of spring Tamar implored her father to let her leave the teeming city and join her noble friends in a nearby village. And her father did not refuse her, but sent her with her handmaid, Maacah, to Abishai in Bethlehem, where the shepherds were pasturing Joram's flocks, bidding her return in three days' time. But his son, Teman, together with three servants, he sent to Sitri on the Carmel to stay there until the first grapes ripened, that he might bring the offering to Jerusalem.

Now Bethlehem, the cradle of Judah's kings, lies south of Jerusalem, built upon a pleasant hump-backed hill and served by numerous wells and fountains whose crystal waters are sweet unto the taste. In this delightful setting the olive trees grow fresh and the vintage vines turn purple beneath the ripening clusters. The hills are girded with delight, and the valleys adorned with a rich embroidery of flowers. The young lambs gambol, the herds of cattle pasture and the land flows with milk and honey; and there King Solomon had hewed him out three cisterns to collect the abundant waters, and made canals to bring them to Jerusalem, his beloved city. The silvery waters are flanked about with pleasing willows, while the turtle-doves and fledgeling pigeons frolic lovingly among the branches. Here Amnon watched over the flocks of Abishai, his father's steward, and was thought to be a shepherd's son. And the local shepherds loved him exceedingly for his beauty and his melodies, for he played upon the harp, and his pleasant songs gladdened their hearts.

And springtime summoned to Bethlehem all the fine young men of Zion with their comely and delightful maidens; and Tamar, too, came into Abishai's house in all her radiance, clad in purple finery. Then she went out with Maacah, her handmaid, to the pastures, and passed the place where Amnon was resting his flock, while all the shepherds gazed at her and marvelled.

אהבת ציון

מאתי

אברהם בן־יקותיאל מאפו

איש קאוונא

⬖⬦⬗

וילנא

בדפוס ר' יוסף ראובן בר' מנחם מן ר א ם

שנת　תרי"ג　לפ"ק

АГАВОТЪ ЦІОНЪ

т. е.

Любовь Ціона, Соч. Авраама Мапу.

ВИЛЬНО,

Въ Типографіи. Р. М. Ромма.

1853.

Title-page of the first edition of *The Love of Zion*

By courtesy of the British Museum

And they said to each other: 'Behold this most beautiful of Zion's daughters!'

But Amnon said to them: 'Woe to the shepherds who raise their eyes too high. Let us rather lower our gaze to our resting flocks, and not dare look upon the noble ladies of the land!' For all that, Amnon followed her with his eyes and marked her steps from afar.

The sun cast its precious light in warm caress upon the pastures, and the running streams gurgled as they flowed. The soft rustling of the leaves as a light breeze played among the branches, the song of the birds, the bleating of the flocks, plainly re-echoing in the hills—all these delights raised the shepherds' spirits, when lo! the piping of a flute drifted across the fields. And Tamar retraced her steps with Maacah, while Amnon, hearing the shepherd's melody, opened his lips in sweet song:

'Your goodly things, O Lord, to rich and poor alike are
    precious,
But not so the worldly pleasures of men,
Of which the rich have greater share than the poor,
Though they are dross and worthless.
But the righteous sun shines forth upon both prince and
    peasant.
Together they delight in the beauties of spring.
The breeze that wafts across the field is of the Lord,
While joy and merriment are all about.
God has given the noisy city to the high-born,
But when spring comes, they cannot bear it more;
Then they yearn for the village and the pasture-lands,
And all the delights of country life.
Leave the coronet with its precious stones
To crown the heads of lords and ladies!
For the roses of the valley are the shepherd's garland
To grace the head of his beloved.'

'Listen, Maacah,' Tamar said to her handmaid, as they sat by the stream some twenty cubits' distance from Amnon the

A M—I

shepherd, 'listen, Maacah, and look, if you have ears to hear and eyes to see.'

And Maacah said: 'Such joy and gladness as the spring-tide scatters in profusion everywhere we walk could scarcely be imagined by those who dwell shut up within the city walls. But come, my mistress, and let us ascend the hill to see the dances. For the merry shepherds and shepherdesses will beat the drums and go out laughing to the dance, while the noble ladies watch them.'

'Let me alone,' Tamar replied. 'Here shall I stay, rooted to this spot. For all the delightful visions which have ever come to me in dreams appear now in broad daylight. And surely I have just seen the youth whom Hananeel, my father, described from his dream. In his entire form not one detail is lacking. Look at the young shepherd, the one who sang. Look at his jet-black locks, and clear-cut build. His skin is white as snow and soft as milk. How rosy are his cheeks, how sweet his voice, how winning his smile! He even grasps a bow in his hand. Only a helmet is required to give him all the splendour of a warrior dressed for battle.'

Then Maacah looked at Amnon, and was overwhelmed by his beauty. So she addressed Tamar: 'My mistress, do not indulge in daydreams lest they play you false, and your visions make you mad. Hananeel is dead, his dream means nothing. And as for the bow he grasps, I can tell you the reason: Not for nothing do the shepherds come to the pastures armed, when spring comes to the pride of the Jordan. For then the lion emerges from the thickets, and the young leopards and other fierce beasts leave their lairs, as the flood waters rise towards them. At this time they ravage the earth about, slaying any man or beast they find alone. Therefore the shepherds arm themselves like warriors. And so, my mistress, let us leave this place, and join the group that is gathered on yonder hill.'

But Tamar gave no heed to Maacah's words. Instead she approached Amnon and addressed him: 'Give me, good youth, the garland of roses which is in your hand, if your heart be generous as your looks are kind.'

As Tamar spoke to him he paled and said: 'Here it is, my mistress, if you but deign to take it from your servant's hand.'

Then Tamar continued: 'I heard you say "The roses of the valley are the shepherd's garland, to grace the head of his beloved." So tell me, then, who is your beloved? For I would fain see her, and give her some gift in exchange for this garland of roses which you meant for her, but which I have taken from you.'

And Amnon lowered his eyes and said: 'I swear, my mistress, that out of the thousands of maidens my eyes have seen I have not yet found my beloved.'

And Tamar answered: 'It would seem, proud youth, that if you seek your beloved among thousands, then must she indeed be rare and choice.'

Then Maacah, her handmaid, took her arm and said: 'Enough, my mistress, let us arise and go. For someone is coming, and it does not befit your honour to stay and bandy words.'

At that moment Uz, the servant of Abishai, drew nigh, and Tamar and Maacah went away.

And Uz asked Amnon: 'What did Jedidiah's daughter say to you?'

And Amnon answered: 'Is she Jedidiah's daughter, and I knew it not? Her words flow sweetly from her lips like drops of morning dew from roses. Shame upon you, Uz! Your coming interrupted her.'

Then Uz replied: 'Amnon, do you aim thus high? Yet Tamar is beautiful indeed, although modest and kind withal. For Zion's daughters are proud. They scorn the poor and needy, and put the oppressed to shame. Not so Tamar! Though her hands be cased in jewels, she opens them wide to the poor, and with kind words heartens the humble. At dawn's first light this morning I saw her in the vineyards, and she seemed to me a lily of delight drenched with the dew of heaven.'

And Amnon said: 'To me she seemed fair as Jerusalem, and lovely as the morning; a noble maiden full of grace, whose modesty vies with her beauty, and in whose soul goodness and charm are one. But how can I describe her beauty? My heart is full, but my tongue can find no words. Yet one thing I will say, Uz. If this maiden were to dwell among the stars of heaven, she would shine forth like the morning star; when she walks through the fields, the roses pale before her.'

And Uz made answer: 'Amnon, no more vain words! Have you forgotten you are a shepherd? Put your mind to your flocks, and guard your sheep—and your tongue!'

But as Tamar walked away from Amnon, she said to Maacah, her handmaid: 'Would that I might pass all my days among these pleasant fields. For the garlands of flowers which grace the heads of the shepherd youths and maidens please me more than the diadems and ornaments that glitter on the foreheads of Zion's daughters; and the shepherd's pipe across the pastures is sweeter to my ear than any harp or lyre resounding in Jerusalem's banquet-halls.'

But Maacah laughed and said: 'This shepherd youth has cast a spell upon the pastures to set you dreaming in broad daylight. Yet I warned you, my mistress, that your daydreams would lead you astray. For even if Hananeel were alive, who would so honour this shepherd as to exalt him to your station?'

And Tamar said: 'Enough of your mockery! He is indeed a shepherd, yet a noble spirit dwells within him, nor can his shepherd clothes conceal it. How sweet his songs, how pleasantly he spoke, and how fine his looks! His eyes are full of charm, his lips—like roses. Were I to bring him to my mother's house, she would agree with me. Nor can you deny that everything about him recalled the youth, whom Hananeel saw in his dream.'

And still speaking of him they reached Abishai's house.

At eventide Amnon gathered his flocks and went to sleep in the shepherds' hut. And Tamar, too, retired to her room to rest. But sleep escaped her and she yearned for day-break, for she planned to return alone to the place where she had seen the youth the previous day, hoping to learn more about him.

That night the lions broke into the sheepfolds and played

havoc with the flocks. And when the shepherds arose and saw that the sheep had been ravaged, they armed themselves with spear and bow, and laid ambushes in the thickets and defiles. But Tamar, who knew nothing of these dread happenings, rose early with the dawn's first light, and walked alone towards the place where she had spoken with the young shepherd. Then suddenly she heard the distant shouts of shepherds who, in full cry, were pursuing a murderous lion that had wrought death and destruction among the flocks and herds, and then vanished without trace. But Tamar, who knew not the cause of all the shouting, paid no heed to it, but gathering flowers as she walked, she made a lovely garland. At last she arrived at the place on the bank of a running brook where she had seen Amnon pasturing his flock the day before, and her heart leaped as she beheld him on the opposite bank, watering his sheep. Like doves above the surface of a pool their eyes met in the reflection of the brook, and joy swelled in their hearts from the lovely picture in the calm waters, for they were ashamed to gaze upon each other face to face. Then Tamar smiled and said: 'I come, good youth, to repay my debt.' And as she spoke she showed him her garland of flowers. And the youth replied: 'But behold, my mistress, a stream of water flows between us, and I cannot reach it.' And Tamar said: 'If your arm is too short I will stretch out mine.' And she threw the garland on to the farther bank, where Amnon stood.

But Amnon shouted in a fearful voice. 'Take care, my mistress.'

And Tamar raised her eyes, and suddenly the fear of death fell upon her, for from the thickets of reeds a murderous lion had emerged. Dreadful to look upon, his hair bristling like nails upon his shoulders, his tail strong as a cedar, his eyes flashing fire, his maw gaping like the grave, from which his tongue flickered like a red flame, thirsting for his victim's blood. Calm and confident he bounded forward, directing his powerful steps towards the sheep across the brook. Then he withdrew a little, tensing himself to spring with one fell leap upon the flock, on which his piercing eyes were fixed. But like a flash of lightning Amnon drew his bow, and a moment later the lion roared once horribly and fell silent, for Amnon's arrow had pierced his heart, and he fell in his tracks not ten paces from Tamar, who had swooned from terror. And Amnon's heart, though it had faced the lion with such courage, melted within him as he saw the beautiful maiden lying senseless. He left his flock and plunged through the brook to stand before Tamar confounded, for she appeared quite lifeless. And he called to her loudly, while the running tears streamed down his cheeks, and shook her gently until her senses returned, and she opened her eyes and saw the lion's corpse, and heard the youth speaking to her thus: 'Be not afraid, my noble lady, have no fear! The danger has passed, the terror is over, for the Lord strengthened your servant's arm, and my arrow pierced his murderous heart, laying him low. See how he lies wallowing in his blood. Look upon him and take courage.'

But Tamar still trembled, her spirit torn between sudden terror and relief. She raised her brimming eyes now to heaven, now to her redeemer, her heart overflowing with gratitude, of which her tongue could frame not a single word. But Amnon continued to soothe her, until her strength returned.

At length she opened her lips and said: 'How wondrous are your works, O Lord! Is there a man who can face death and life in a single moment and remain unmoved? Yet I, a gentle and timid maid, have seen them both at once, and shall I restrain my spirit? Behold the lion was upon me, terrible to look upon, with his dread fangs and razor claws, his fierce eyes searching to rip my heart and crush my bones.'

Then Tamar grasped Amnon's right hand and continued: 'But your arm and your right hand, dear youth, saved me from him. Like a comrade in distress, a rescuing angel, you rushed to my aid. Verily your kindness is too great to be repaid with thanks.'

But Amnon answered: 'Salvation is of the Lord. He it was who gave me strength to strike down this wild beast. Rise, then, and bless your Redeemer.'

And Tamar asked his name.

And the shepherd replied: 'My name is Amnon.'

And Tamar continued: 'Then, Amnon, I shall call you by your name. But I pray you, Amnon, please accept these bracelets from my arm as a token of remembrance, not as a reward for your deed, but that you may remember my name, and not forget me. But my father shall reward you, and his generous hand will raise you on high. For it is not fitting for such a fine young man to live among the sheep-folds and to mingle with the lowly, squandering your strength upon the wild beasts, and wasting your sweet words on the trees of the field. My father is Jedidiah, a nobleman in Judah, and rich withal, and he has the power to exalt your horn in honour.'

But Amnon answered: 'Do not entreat me, my mistress, to take this token of remembrance from you. Rather remember that I am a shepherd, and if I remember you, I shall forget the world and all its fullness.' And as he spoke the tears trickled down his cheeks.

And Tamar said: 'These tears that shine like pearls upon your cheeks bear witness that you will not forget me even as I have never forgotten you.'

'But where have you seen me, noble lady?' Amnon asked her in amazement.

'In my dreams,' Tamar replied with a charming smile. 'But the Lord has granted me this day to see you in the flesh.'

And Amnon said: 'Forgive me, my mistress, but I do not understand your riddle.'

And Tamar laughed and answered: 'Then when you come to Jerusalem to celebrate the Feast of Weeks, come to my father's house, for there you may hope to glory in the company of warriors, and take delight in the prophets, the disciples of the Lord, who partake of the good things in my father's house. There you will understand my riddle. See! I charge you by the roes, and by the hinds of the field, to fulfil my desire, for perhaps your own desire requires it. And now rejoice in peace and remember Tamar, who will await you longingly, and who will never forget her Amnon.'

While she was speaking Maacah, her handmaid, came in

search of her, and shuddered as she beheld the lion's corpse. Then Tamar told her how the shepherd had saved her.

And Maacah said: 'You have brought this upon yourself.'

But Tamar made her swear not to speak badly of her to her father, but to tell him that the youth had saved her life; and Maacah, who hoped herself to find what Tamar sought, rejoiced to hear that Tamar wished to bring him beneath her own roof. So both of them set off to return to Abishai's house. And Amnon skinned the lion to make a basket-saddle for his ass, while Tamar glanced back at him ever and again.

And it came to pass one day that Uz visited the pastures and found Amnon sitting wrapped in thought, watching a lily withering beneath the scorching heat and speaking thus: 'How lovely you are, my soft and tender lily, when dawn's first light steals upon you, when your cup is brimming with the dew of heaven, and even the great trees look enviously upon you! How beautiful you appear, my lovely one, in the light of the morning, when the clear drops of dew sparkle on your sweet petals, and you drink your fill and in good time blossom forth in joy. But now the scorching heat has smitten you, the dew of heaven has dried within you, and your face is wan, your bloom has withered, and you have become an object to be pitied. Thus even the plants of the field can teach us, and from whatever our eyes behold we can draw a moral. The heavens stretch an open book in front of us, while the earth, and all its host, spreads out its lesson before our very eyes. The word of God is stamped upon it, telling us: Read in this great book all the days of your life, for only then shall you act wisely and with understanding! For like this lily a man blooms and flowers in the morning of his youth, until love blossoms in his heart, and all its delights combine to quench his splendour, for it scorches his spirit within him, till it withers away without finding what it seeks.'

'What ails you, Amnon?' Uz inquired of him. 'For some days past you have seemed strange, your face is changed, your habits altered, although I know not why. You haunt the thickets of the forest like some lone bird, or like a stag stand languishing at every pool. As soon as the sun begins to shine upon the pastures even unto the waning of the day you skip up hill, down dale without knowing what you seek. And when I leave the flocks with you, the sheep scatter from our pastures and stray in all directions, while you heed them not. For your heart is full of fancies, and you mouth fine words beyond my understanding.'

'Listen, Uz,' Amnon replied. 'Listen to these wondrous tidings. You surely know Tamar, and how I scarcely dared to think of her; I saved her from the murderous lion that our shepherds were pursuing—its carcase lies hidden in yonder grove—and now Tamar has entreated me with love to dwell within her father's house. Therefore do I wander about thinking of the honour which Tamar has promised for me.'

And Uz was amazed at what he heard, and said: 'Thus you did and told no one! I grieve for you, Amnon. For though such thoughts may enchant you now like doves with golden feathers, yet in the end like the ravens of the valley they will pick bare your youthful bones. Will you pursue the stork into the heavens? Will you run after the fleet hind upon the lofty hills? Rather forget and lay aside such cares!'

But Uz related it to Abishai, and Abishai was astounded and afraid. So he sent Amnon to Bozrah to buy sheep. And when Jedidiah sent a message summoning him, they sent back word that Amnon was in Bozrah.

CHAPTER 5

Now Teman went to Sitri in the Carmel at his father's bidding, and Sitri greeted him joyfully. Next morning they arose early and together entered the vineyards. The dawn shone brightly over the Carmel and the vineyards resounded with shouting and song. Young men and maids were gathering the grapes, loudly singing songs of wine and love. And Teman led his three servants to the choicest of the vineyards and said: 'Pay close heed to every branch that is tied with rushes, for that is a sign of its holiness; and gather only the fruit thereof, for they are the first offerings for the priests. Look at that fruitful vine, striking her roots in the furrows, spreading out her tendrils over the hills, and showing her abundant blessing for all to see. Her branches bend beneath the weight of the clusters of juicy, ripening grapes. How lovely is their rich, dull glow! Look at the ripe figs and pomegranates peeping through the fresh-green leaves that cover them. They seem almost to plead with me to bring them to the Temple. They, too, have been marked out as first-fruits, whose juice and new wine belong to them that dwell with the Lord. See that fine olive-tree, whose stateliness befits his splendid fruit, all bursting with rich oil, a sweet offering for the Lord, who pours His blessing on our land.'

Then Teman turned to the gatherers and said: 'Take care lest you strip them bare! Eat of the grapes as you will, but be not so uncharitable as to hinder them that come here to forget their burden and their sorrow. Drive them not away and vex them not. For who knows what may come? Perhaps our sons and daughters may suffer thirst and hunger, and go seeking sustenance for their souls in fields and vineyards that belong to others. Therefore leave the gleanings, for they are the levy which we raise for the Lord, who has sent these blessings upon us.'

And the hands of the young men and maidens flew dexterously, shouting and laughing as they worked. The boys and girls emptied the full baskets into pitchers, which the men carried on their shoulders, bearing them to the wine-presses. And here two husbandmen were talking, and one said: 'The wine is clear and red as the dew of heaven in the rosy glow of morning.' And his fellow answered: 'It is like wine brought to the Temple, all of it sweeter than choice fruit.' And opposite them they that pressed the grapes shouted 'Hurrah! Good wine rejoices God and man; for some of it will be poured upon the altar, and some will remind old men of the joys of their youth, and make old friends delight in one another.'

The time for the midday meal drew nigh. The tired youths and maidens lay down to rest in every corner of the vineyard, laughing and refreshing their spirits with merry, innocent jests.

Here a youth begins to climb a palm, grasping the panicles with his hands, but suddenly losing his foothold so that he falls down amidst laughter: there a maiden pursues a youth whose words have angered her, holding a bunch of grapes to chasten him. She catches him and squashes the grapes on his cheek, so that his face is stained with purple, while the onlookers laugh aloud. Thus the noise and clamour continued until the meal was ready.

Meanwhile Teman walked about the vineyards in all directions, and suddenly among the branches of the vines he chanced upon a maiden gleaning the remnants of the vineyard, paying no heed to the noisy frolics of the young men; and when she smiled, it hovered on her ruby lips like a gentle wind upon a lily of Sharon, enhancing the splendour of her beauty and her fine looks; but as the smile vanished her gentle eyes shone with a soft and lovely radiance. And Teman stood watching her, astounded at her beauty, the like of which he had never seen, unable to take his eyes off her for a moment, or move a step. Then with a sigh he said: 'This lovely prize will fall to the lot of some lowly fellow, while for me the Lord has destined honour, wealth, and the daughter of some Judaean nobleman. Yet give all those things, O Lord, to whomsoever you please. Grant honour to them that rule, wealth to the righteous, a noble maiden to them that love ornaments, silks and embroideries; but grant me this maiden, whom I would not change for a royal princess in all her finery. Grant me a plot of land and a few vines from your wide earth and some little hut to dwell in with her alone, and there would be no happiness like mine.'

He was still sunk in thought, nor had he yet asked the girl her name and parentage, when one of his servants drew nigh, requesting him in the name of all the harvesters and husbandmen to return; for the men would not sit down to eat before Teman had blessed the bread and wine, and before they had blessed him in the Lord's name, for Sitri was not in the vineyard. So Teman went to them and fulfilled their request. Then he returned to the same place—but the maiden had vanished. And he sought her throughout the groves, but found her not;

and on the next day he sought her everywhere—in vain. And Teman was very sad, and the third day passed without relieving his despair.

But on the fourth day Teman set out hunting on the Carmel with two servants, when suddenly a fine stag rushed past with neck outstretched, as though exulting in the great antlers which crowned his head to make him king of the forest. Their footsteps had frightened him from his lair and he fled wildly for his life, changing his course and swerving to throw his pursuers off his track, and glancing behind him as he ran. But instead of fleeing away through open country, he turned into the thickets of the wood. Then Teman ordered his servants to descend to the edge of the Carmel forest, while he went on alone. Then losing his way he shouted loudly to his servants to return, but no one answered; so he stumbled on, knowing not whether to turn right or left. When suddenly he caught the flicker of a white robe of someone walking in the distance, and he ran like a hind towards it. And as he reached the place, he found the very maiden whom he had seen in the vineyard, radiant as the dawn between the thickets of the forest. She was walking near a little hut, built in a crevice in the rock, and when she saw Teman, she drew back in fear.

But Teman said to her: 'Be not afraid, my lovely one! One thing only do I ask of you. Now that the Lord has let me find you, give me back what you have taken from me.'

'O my master,' the maiden answered while the tears rolled down her cheek. 'Do not impute such a sin to me! God forbid that your handmaid should take anything that is not hers. These last four days I have been in your vineyards, but I ate not of the clusters, and took nothing except the gleanings. For the gleanings of the grape and wheat harvests are all that your handmaid and her mother have for sustenance.'

'And who is your mother?' Teman asked her. 'And of what tribe your father?'

'My mother is a Philistine woman,' the maiden answered. 'And though I never knew my father, my mother knows his tribe.'

Then Teman asked her where her mother dwelt, and the maiden replied: 'She dwells in the hut, built in this crevice in the rock. But she has gone away and will return only in three days' time. But tell me, my lord, why have you so frightened me in asking me to return what I have never taken?'

And Teman said: 'You have taken much—more than any gold can buy. Give me back, my lovely hind, give me back the power of sleep and peace of mind, for since I saw you, both these things have left me.'

And the girl was confounded by his words, for she did not understand their portent, so she answered: 'What, then, did you see in your handmaid?'

'The earth and all the fullness thereof,' Teman replied, and taking the ring from his finger he gave it to her, saying: 'Tell me your name!'

And the maiden answered: 'Here I am called Shoshana.'*

Then Teman said: 'Your name becomes you. But know, gentle Shoshana, that like the jewel set in this ring, your precious image is embedded in my heart. And one of two things must come to pass. Either I shall exalt you to dwell with me in marble palaces, or I must descend to live with you in this hut.'

And the maiden stood amazed and gazed at Teman without grasping his meaning. Then finally she said: 'How good and kind you are, my lord, but I dwell here with my mother, and the hut is too small for you to dwell with us. And why should you leave a pleasant palace to dwell in this deserted place? But come, I pray you, in three days' time, and my mother shall hear your request, for I know not what to answer.'

And Teman could contain himself no longer, but kissed her and said: 'You are right, gentle maiden. I shall speak with your mother. But show me now, I pray you, the way from this place.'

And Shoshana showed him the path that would lead him to Sitri, and he left her to return homewards. But his soul yearned impatiently for the passing of the days.

* Rose.

And on the second day Sitri prepared the first fruits of the grape harvest, and urged Teman to bring them to Jerusalem. So they placed the choice fruit in gold and silver baskets, garnishing them about with turtle-doves and fledgeling pigeons, and they loaded the baskets on young asses and set off early in the morning. And behold an ox walked on cloven hoofs before them, glorying in his horns covered with gold and garlanded with olive leaves, which sparkled like a crown upon his head, marking him out to be king of the beasts of the field. For many a harvest had depended on his strength, and by his aid man had opened up the earth, turning the furrows behind him. But now his heavy labour was done, and he cried peace upon the hills and valleys from which he had brought forth abundant crop, making food for others. For his was a holy path to Jerusalem, there to end his life, but in dying, bringing joy to God and man, giving his blood and fat to God, and his soft flesh as dainties for his lords.

And Teman addressed his servants when they had gone some little distance from Carmel, saying: 'Proceed upon the way, but slowly. I, meanwhile, shall go back to Carmel, for something must still be done, and towards evening I shall return.'

And Teman rode upon his mule as though cloud-borne to come to Shoshana's dwelling place. But when he reached it, alas! he found not what he sought, only an old woman, who gave him the precious jewel which was set in his ring, and said: 'Thus the Philistine woman did say, who dwelt here, in her daughter's name: "The jewel is sundered from the ring, nor is there any force that can join it again!"'

Then Teman wrung his hands and cried: 'Whither went the two women? Tell me, I pray you, and whatever you ask shall be yours.'

And the old woman replied: 'I know no more than you whither they went. I have told you exactly what the Philistine woman bade me say. But one thing she told me, that to this place she would return no more.'

Then Teman set off after his servants sore at heart, brooding upon the meaning of the affair. And he overtook his servants, and together they journeyed to Jerusalem. And Jedidiah made offering of the basket of first fruits according to the law, while Teman remained sad and angry, though he revealed not to his parents the cause thereof.

THE PLOT OF 'THE GUILT
OF SAMARIA'

IN the reign of the evil King Ahaz of Judah there lives a certain Uzziel, an outlaw in a mountain cave in Lebanon, attended only by one faithful servant. A god-fearing nobleman of Jerusalem, he has incurred the wrath of King Ahaz because of his marriage to Miriam, the daughter of Shamir, a warrior of Ephraim. Ahaz himself loved Miriam in his youth, but she could not return his love because of her aversion to his evil practices. So long as Joram was king of Judah, Uzziel and Miriam lived happily, and she bore him a son. But as soon as Ahaz ascended the throne, Uzziel was forced to flee. After wandering through Moab and Egypt, and encountering many misfortunes, he finally came to Lebanon and fortified himself in his mountain fortress, where he is now regarded as a lone bandit.

One day Manoah, the Hebronite, whose estates are close at hand, overhears Uzziel in prayer, and realizing that he is far from being a bandit, approaches him and recognizes him to be Uzziel. Manoah informs him of all that has transpired in Judah and Ephraim since his flight, and brings him to his own house under the name of Eliada. There he meets Jehosheba, the widow of Elkanah, the king's minister whom Zichri, the Ephraimite warrior, slew in battle. She is now a close friend of Uzziel's wife, Miriam. He also meets Hannah, Manoah's wife (whom he married after the death of his first wife Noah), Zephaniah his son and Shulamit, Noah's daughter.

From Jehosheba Uzziel learns that Shamir has sacrificed his son to Moloch to erase all trace of Uzziel, and that Miriam has adopted a foundling as her son and called him Eliphelet. But Uzziel knows that Eliphelet is his real son, the one who was sacrificed having been substituted for him. Jehosheba then describes the war which Judah waged against Ephraim and Aram, in which her husband, together with the king's son, Maaseiah, and Azrikam the king's steward were killed by

אשמת שמרון

נכבדות מדבר בו בימי אחז מלך יהודה ופקח
בן רמליהו והושע בן אלה מלכי ישראל

מאת

אברהם בן־יקותיאל מאפו

זִכְרוּ מֵרָחוֹק אֶת ה'
וִירוּשָׁלַיִם תַּעֲלֶה עַל לְבַבְכֶם
(ירמיה נ'א נ')

חלק ראשון

——◆◆◆——

ווילנא

בדפוס ר' יוסף ראובן בר' מנחם מן ראם

שנת תרכ'ו לפ'ק

———

АШМАѲЪ-ШОМРОНЪ,

т. е.

Козни Самаріи. Соч. А. Мапу.

——◆◆◆——

ВИЛЬНО.

Въ типографіи Р. М. Ромма.

1865.

Title-page of the first edition of *The Guilt of Samaria*
By courtesy of the Bodleian Library, Oxford

Zichri. In this battle Maaseiah had placed Eliphelet on the most dangerous front, regarding him as an obstacle to his love for Kezia, Elkanah's daughter. But Eliphelet had fought and captured an amazon-like warrioress, Reumah, whom Keturah had borne to Zichri. Having sworn to love only the man who could overcome her in battle, Reumah had intervened on behalf of Eliphelet after the total defeat of Judah's army, and sent him to Jerusalem to return to her with his entire household. But Eliphelet, who loves Kezia, has not returned, and has been sent by Ahaz as an envoy to Assyria.

Jehosheba, however, plans to wed Eliphelet to Shulamit and sets out to Gilead to intercept him. But her servant Abishag reveals her plan to the villains Omri and Zimri, who inform Keturah, who, in turn, informs her daughter Reumah. On that same day, which is a festival at Beth-El, Reumah issues a challenge to the Ephraimite warriors to do battle with her in a tournament. The challenge is accepted by Daniel, Azrikam's son, disguised under the name of Ammihud. Daniel is searching for a maiden who showed him compassion when he was taken captive after the disastrous battle, but whom he has seen only once. Unknown to him, she is Shulamit, Noah's daughter. But he is also seeking an opportunity to take revenge on Zichri for his father's murder, hence his acceptance of Reumah's challenge.

Reumah is informed of her adversary's likeness to Daniel and decides to use him to wean Shulamit's affections from Eliphelet. She sends him with his servant Joach in search of her, but they are separated at night in the hills of Lebanon. As dawn breaks Daniel hears Shulamit praying to God, and they are joyfully reunited. Daniel learns that she is the daughter of Elkanah, and they retire to her home, where they are joined by Joach, who arrives with Uzziel.

Three days later Daniel sets off to return to Reumah, still bent upon revenge, and also in the hope of saving other Judaeans who are in her power. On the way he meets Eliphelet, who is returning from Assyria with rich treasure. Eliphelet has just saved the life of Hephzibah, a former wife of Zichri but a friend of Judah. She had been attacked by an Ethiopian at the instigation of Keturah and Reumah, as a prelude to an attack on Miriam. It transpires that Uzziel had many years previously saved Hephzibah's life from a similar attack by the father of this Ethiopian.

Near Jerusalem Eliphelet meets Manoah bringing Uzziel, disguised as Eliada, to serve as the steward of Miriam's estates, and gives him a letter for Miriam, disclosing that the king has destined Kezia for Daniel. Uzziel and Miriam are overjoyed at meeting after so many years of separation, but dare not reveal their secret. Meanwhile Magdiel, who had himself aspired to the stewardship of Miriam's estates, informs Eliphelet that Eliada and Miriam are meeting secretly at night. Unaware that Eliada is Miriam's husband, Eliphelet leaves Jerusalem in a rage, and is captured by the Edomites, who plan to sacrifice him to their gods. He is rescued by one of Miriam's agents, who is unaware, however, of his identity.

Meanwhile Uzziel receives a warning that his presence has been discovered and is forced to flee once again, leaving Miriam even more disconsolate than formerly. The irony of her plight is increased by the death of King Ahaz and the ascension of the righteous Hezekiah, who listens readily to Isaiah's teachings. For she realizes that her husband could well return to Jerusalem and live in peace. In Samaria, on the other hand, licentiousness and vice are rampant, every form of idolatry is practised, while the righteous suffer persecution.

The fame of Zichri and his daughter Reumah has reached its zenith. Daniel is imprisoned in Zichri's palace, and a rich ransom is placed on his life. Shulamit, too, is abducted from Manoah's house and carried there. But Reumah nurses hatred against her father, Zichri, who has engineered her mother's death, and so she furnishes Shulamit with the sword of her father Elkanah, which Zichri had taken after killing him. Daniel manages to secure this sword and wounds Zichri when he enters Shulamit's room.

Meanwhile Uzziel has come to Samaria to win converts back to the true religion, and there he meets Eliphelet, who is endeavouring to redeem Reumah's prisoners. Uzziel reveals to Eliphelet that he is his father and they are reconciled. With the help of Sharezer, the prince of Assyria, they rescue the captives. But Samaria, after the overthrow and exile of her king and nobles, is plunged into a state of dreadful confusion, and punished for her many sins.

The heroes return triumphantly to Jerusalem to celebrate the Feast of Passover. Uzziel is united to Miriam, Eliphelet to Kezia and Daniel to Shulamit. With Miriam's consent Uzziel takes the unhappy Jehosheba as a second wife. The king rewards Uzziel with rich estates at En-Gedi, to which he and his household retire to spend their remaining years far from the city's tumult!

THE GUILT OF SAMARIA

CHAPTER 1

IN the days when Ahaz reigned in Judah, and Pekah son of Remaliah and Hoshea son of Elah were the kings in Israel, the prophets grew hoarse with rebuking the refractory people and wearied themselves with appeals to their erring and presumptuous hearts. In those evil times Ephraim knew only rebellion, and Judah deceit. Ephraim offered up his sons for slaughter, and Judah sacrificed his choicest offspring through the fire to Moloch. Thus did King Ahaz, and his people followed in his ways. The law disappeared out of Zion, while truth and honesty fled from Samaria's gates, to hide among the clefts of the hills, and in the crevices of the rocks. Righteousness dwelt only in the forest, and Faith in caves.

But to the end of time righteousness shall not perish, nor shall wickedness and folly cease. For where the shadows lurk, there light is found. Thus did the Lord create the world and thus did he establish it, summer joined to winter, night ever linked with morning. And even thus did the Lord create man, whose heart is always full of evil inclination, while his good sense protects him like an angel, that he follow not his rebellious desires. Its light is like the rainbow in a day of dark cloud, fashioned in ancient times as witness to the covenant of peace, to remind men that the Lord creates light and darkness, and from on high makes peace between them as they strive with one another. From the lowliest earth to the highest star the splendour of his work appears in everything created in his name and for his glory. For his actions are all weighed, and he will not destroy the good for evil's sake, but he takes forth the precious from the vile, the pure from the corrupt; and from a perverse and crooked generation he separates the pure of heart, those who are wise and know the Lord, who shine through the darkness like a rainbow through the darkest night. And the soul of man is like the light of God, searching the innermost recesses of the heart. And even when Israel and

134

Judah broke all bounds, and profaned the glory of his might, and the pride of Jacob lay prostrate before the abominations of idolatry, even then the light of God shone forth upon the righteous, and the pure of heart glowed like precious stones upon God's earth. And when Ahaz closed the portals of the Lord, Lebanon threw wide her gates that all the faithful might enter therein. And there they served the Lord by torch-light, and in the secret places of the forest paid homage to the Holy One of Israel.

In the remotest mountains of Lebanon, which form the northern boundary of the tribe of Naphtali where the Hermonites dwell in bands, the peak of Amana towers aloft. At the foot of this mountain there unfolds a valley, the most beautiful and lovely in all the mountain ranges round about. And from the rocks rivulets gush forth and stream into this vale, where the limpid brooks unite and flow beneath the ground until they emerge from the bosom of the earth to form a mighty river—the river Jordan.

The dew of Hermon still lingers mistily over the valleys, enveloping the bushes, thickets and pasture-lands, as the dawn stretches across the mountains, lighting in gold the glory of Lebanon and the great proud trees, whose roots dig deep into the soil while their tops grope towards heaven. These mighty cedars are ancient as the earth which carries them, and their leafy tops spread out and intertwine with one another. Their foliage forms a shady grotto even at noontide, and provides a nesting place for every sort of bird that sings the praise of Lebanon to the Lord. The ear can never weary of their sweet song and pleasant melody. And the mountain tops re-echo the roars of savage beasts; for there the lions and panthers have their lairs, and the soul thrills fearfully to the sound of their mingled cries. These mountains drip with the juice of the abounding vines that bend beneath the burden of their clusters. Even the earth breathes myrrh and frankincense, while the scent of spices creeps into the nostrils of the traveller. And hence the phrase 'it bears the scent of Lebanon', for Lebanon is shrouded in delight, and how much more so when the dawn breaks over it, laying bare such beauty that the heart cries out in joy.

The summer was drawing to a close. It was the month before Ethanim,* when the sun scorches the land and the fullness thereof, giving no respite from its heat. Wherefore travellers would arise at the first watch to journey through the morning mists. At that very time three travellers arose, who had lodged safely among the Hermonites. They were returning from Damascus, the land of their captivity, where Rezin, king of Aram, had brought the great captivity of Judah, throwing their princes in prison, but freeing the poor to return to their own land, that they might relate the sorrows of the princes held captive in iron fetters, and thereby hasten their redemption with rich ransom. And these three of the captivity of Damascus were of the poor of the land of Judah, and traversed the way of the Hermonites on camel-back, their faces set towards Jerusalem. They were accompanied by the servants of a rich man of that place who came to send them on their way; and all were well armed against the terrors of the night, for the wild beasts of Lebanon abounded at that season, and the lions could be heard snarling for their prey, while the mists of dew that billowed down upon them from Hermon blotted out the paths from before their eyes. These three impoverished men—one from Adullam, the second from Lachish and the third from Ziph—had no portion or inheritance in their own land, but found their sustenance in Jerusalem, serving in one of the houses of the great. And just as in times of peace they had beheld the grandeur of their master's house, so had they seen its pride overthrown in war and known its shame. Wherefore the Hermonite servants questioned them on what they had seen and what they knew of the dire destruction which had but lately befallen Judah.

'All three of us are of the poor of the land'—answered the man of Adullam, 'and who are we to record a nation's story? My birth was lowly, but I beheld the highest in the land when I served in the house of Azrikam, who was the steward of

* The seventh month.

King Ahaz, and in whose house I witnessed pride and grandeur.
For Elkanah, that was next to the king, would come there
with the lady Jehosheba his wife, and with their daughter,
Kezia, the loveliest of Zion's maidens. And these two princes of
Judah, who stood at the head of all the noble families, thought
to join their houses in marriage. For Kezia, the daughter of
Elkanah, that was next to the king, was destined for Daniel, the
son of Azrikam my master, the steward of the king. But
Maaseiah, the son of King Ahaz, stood between them like a
rock. And what was the latter end of these high, exalted
figures? Alas! Their doom was sealed, for Maaseiah the king's
son, and Elkanah, that was next to the king, and Azrikam,
the king's steward, were all slain by Zichri, the hero of Ephraim, in the war of the allied kings, Pekah son of Remaliah
and Rezin king of Aram, against Judah. Zichri smote these
three pillars of strength and shook the foundations of the land,
for one hundred and twenty thousand valiant sons of Judah
fell smitten before the might of Remaliah. Alas! The land of
Judah is withered and lies mourning.'

'Verily, it is so'—the man of Lachish replied. 'Many homes
lie desolate in Zion. Do you not know, have you not heard,
how the noble Joram met his end, a captive of the Philistines,
while Naame, his beloved wife, ransacked his treasures, plun-
dered his wealth and set fire to his estate for jealousy of
Haggith, her adversary? And the flames consumed his children
saving only one, Haggith's son, who alone survived like a
brand plucked from the fire. Then Naame fled from her vile
crime, and escaped to her lover. Five years have passed since
that dread deed, but is it not enough to desecrate the land?'

'Misery has indeed befallen the great in Judah,' the man of
Ziph continued. 'Do you not know the noble lady Miriam
who dwells in Zion? I know her story well, for Achsah, my
sister, is a handmaid in her house. This Miriam, who is both
gracious and wealthy, inherited the fortune of her mother
Deborah, to the great chagrin of Shamir her father, a bitter
enemy of Judah and the house of David, for he is descended
from Ephraim's kings. And he was sorely vexed to see his

daughter Miriam following in the footsteps of Deborah, her mother, and loving her people Judah. And his fury increased when Miriam fell in love with Uzziel, the son of a Judaean nobleman, a scion of the house of Uzziah. But Miriam loved him both for his beauty and his nobility, for he was of the royal blood. Then in his anger against his daughter Miriam and Uzziel her husband, Shamir swore a secret oath to blot out their memory for ever. Which oath he fulfilled, for he sacrificed their offspring to Moloch, and caused Uzziel to flee to the land of Moab in the early days of Ahaz's reign. And the lady Miriam has lived a miserable widow's life these fifteen years.'

'No need to tell me that,' replied the man of Lachish. 'When Jedidiah, the ruler of the king's substance, sent me to the country of the Philistines to inquire after the treacherous Naame and to trace her footsteps, at that same time Miriam summoned me to her, and implored me search for news of her husband Uzziel, who had left Moab and gone to the Philistines, and from there to Egypt. Yet neither the money which she gave me nor my toil were ought avail. Would that I might have found him, for now I would be rich. Verily, there is no end to the wealth which Miriam received from Deborah her mother, and in bereavement and widowhood her whole desire is to perform good deeds. She is a refuge for abandoned orphans, and a shelter for the heroes of the war. And one orphan in particular, a handsome and valiant youth named Eliphelet, has she adopted. And by virtue of her compassion and love for him, she has made him a place among the young noblemen favoured by the king, and regards him as her son.'

'That is all mere hearsay,' answered the man of Adullam. 'All Eliphelet's greatness came from Maaseiah, the king's son, whose weapon-bearer he was, just as I bore the weapons of Daniel, son of Azrikam, the king's steward. But listen now, and wonder, for Kezia, the daughter of Elkanah, that was next to the king, the most beautiful of Zion's maidens and a joy to behold—this Kezia would pay no heed to Daniel, my master, comely though he was, nor would she deign to notice even Maaseiah, the son of King Ahaz, but raised her eyes to Eliphelet, whom Miriam adopted, against the will of Elkanah her father. But he, together with his friend Azrikam, the king's steward, and Maaseiah, the king's son, were slain all three by Zichri, the hero of Ephraim. And Daniel, my young master, lies in prison in Damascus. Soon will he hear that Kezia, daughter of Elkanah, has fallen the fair lot of the low-born Eliphelet. For a kind of madness has beset the great ones of the land. Thus the lady Jehosheba, Kezia's mother, used to say, and thus I too observed when I passed through Gilead on the road to captivity with Daniel, my master, son of the king's steward. For there our captors let us rest, and there a maiden saw him, a lovely maiden beautiful as Kezia, daughter of Elkanah, in all her radiance. She saw him from afar and wept for the wanderer. Daniel, too, espied her and waved his hand to her in love, until our cruel captors let us enjoy the sight no longer. Yet the memory of this girl weighed heavily upon his spirit in the land of his captivity, for her image was ever before his eyes, though he had never seen her else and even her name was hidden from him, so that he would refer to her as "his heart's desire". Such is the folly that has overcome the great ones of the earth.'

In this wise the sons of Judah, returning from Damascus, the land of their captivity, related their stories to the servants who had come to send them on their way, and still talking they reached the peak of Amana. And there the servants stopped and listened intently to the cry of a stag. And one of the servants said to his fellow: 'Go, tell our master that the lion of Amana still lurks in his lair, and bid him arm his men and bring them to some fastness on the mountain, for he shall surely fall into our hands, and all the iniquity he has wrought in Lebanon shall descend upon his head. I pity the young deer that has fallen prey to him, and the poor doe that will yearn for her lost one. For these two young deer were the delight of Shulamit, our master's daughter, and they would eat out of her hand, and brought her comfort in her time of mourning for her mother. And now the one young deer will serve as food for this man of blood.'

Then the men of Judah inquired of them concerning the matter, and one of the servants related that a murderous robber had found a lair on the peak of Amana since the beginning of spring, and was plundering Lebanon like a ravening lion. He had made his home high up upon the crag where even the wild beasts could not ascend, and on a nearby spur of rock a tawny leopard stood guard over his lair. For the man of blood was a sorcerer, and even the wild beasts quaked before him. And thus had he lived for several months: 'He rises early in search of prey, and returns late at night to his hiding place, nor has anyone of us looked upon his face. And just as he is, so is the servant who accompanies him. But my master has resolved to put an end to the dread of this tyrant, and to storm his lair this very morning. Then shall his bloody deeds recoil upon him, he shall bear the penalty for his evil ways, and the wrath of Lebanon shall descend upon his head.'

When he had finished speaking the three men of Judah thanked the servants for their night's lodging and the provision for the journey, and having blessed them rode off upon their way to their own land.

As dawn broke over the peak of Amana, behold a man, clad in a coarse garment, appeared upon the rocky spur which even the wild beasts could not ascend, and stood listening to the voices of the servants talking far below. Then hastily he returned to a cave hewn from the living rock and composed of two vaults, the outer one for himself, and the inner one for his master. In this vault a hole had been driven through the wall which by day was covered with a plank of cedarwood to ward off the fierce heat of summer. But now the aperture was open facing the east, letting in the scent of Lebanon together with the morning light, which illumined everything inside. The floor was covered with the skins of wild beasts, and the walls were hung with every sort of weapon: bows, spears, lances and javelins, even a great sword encased in its sheath—a sure sign that this hunter was also a man of war. Outside this dwelling on a spur of rock a dreadful tawny leopard stood motionless. The outlaw had killed it and stuffed its skin, and set it on the crag to terrify whoever might be so brave as to assay the man who had overcome wild beasts in strength and courage. But even without the terror of wild beasts, this refuge was secure; for the sheer cliffs were its rampart, and those who lived there went up and down a ladder of rope. This ladder was securely fastened with an iron peg, and was lowered at need. And the servant, who attended to the outlaw, entered the vault and took down two powerful bows from the wall, to be ready for his master's coming.

Yet at that moment his master was not as a man prepared for battle, for every morning he prayed to the Lord. And even now, when his enemies were about to assault his lair, he stood in contemplation. He was a handsome man in the prime of life, and his thoughts were clearly depicted on his face as his spirit welled up and cried:

'O Almighty, whose ways are exalted above the mountains of God, and whose mercy is greater than the resounding seas, look down upon this lone soul that pleads with you, turn your face to one who is downtrodden and lost, who cries to you with stricken heart: why do I see evil strutting above erect and fearless, while righteousness hides stealthily in the crevices of the rocks; or wickedness enthroned in marble palaces, while honesty lurks in the thickets for fear of the sin of the land and the evil of its inhabitants? Wherefore, O Lord my God, did you grant me tranquillity and joy in my youth, to torture me in mature years with memories of my beloved, with long exile and with fears? For one brief space I witnessed life and happiness with my beloved Miriam. She sat in marble palaces at my right hand, and everything I beheld about me was clothed in delight, all Zion and her assemblies. But alas, my time of joy was all too short, and how long have been the years of affliction! For your anger, O Lord my God, has been raised against me all this time, and you have tossed me about through foreign lands—Moab, Philistia and Egypt. And you have sated me with wanderings even as in the days of the kingdom of Ahaz. And now you have set me on this mountain peak like a black stone, to fill my soul with dread. Still have you not restored me to tranquillity and honour, for you have decreed the measure of my sufferings, O God of wrath. But in spite of all my misfortunes is the cup not yet full? Woe to me that am cut off from my people, from Miriam, my gracious wife and my soul's delight, and from Eliphelet, our beloved child, whom our hands lifted from our pleasant garden to plant amongst the thickets of the forest, that they might protect him from the evil man who sought to extirpate him root and branch. For those dear ones I have raised my hands in prayer all the days of my wanderings, and even today I lift my thoughts to them from the Jordan and the Hermon. Indeed, O Lord God, You have afflicted me sore, yet not consumed me utterly; and that is a sign that you have spared me for the sake of my beloved ones, and that I shall look upon them again when the time is ripe. But when will that time come? How long shall I be a stranger in the land? How long shall my way be wrapped in darkness? Behold, I am blown about like stubble on the mountains, afraid of Judah, fearful of Ephraim. Alas! I have been fearful, afraid and blown about these sixteen years. I came hither like a wayfarer that turns aside to tarry for a night, and chose the peak of Amana for my abode. And yet I have dwelt here full four months in vain. I was almost at peace, and thought I would remain here until your anger, O Lord God, had passed. But you have fixed the years of my affliction, and so affliction and sorrow will discover me wheresoever I be. O Lord, who looks into men's hearts, surely you have searched in mine, and know that I fear you. But why do I tremble at the sound of every falling leaf, for my heart is in my mouth continually? I hunt my prey with bow and arrow, return and lay me down to rest inside my abode, and behold, I am beset with fears of men who know me not, who plan to storm my lair and hunt me like a wild man. When, O Lord of my Salvation, will you bring my redemption, return me to Miriam, my wife, for whom I yearn, and to Eliphelet, my son, my delight and comfort in all my years of wandering? Shall God abandon me for ever?

Will you not set me free, for behold, the year of Jubilee has come!

'You, yourself, O Lord, decreed the year of Jubilee, the year of redemption in the land. But my redemption has not come. Liberty is in the land, but I am like a wandering bird. For you, O Lord, say to my soul: "Fly to the mountains, fly from the hatred of Shamir, your father-in-law, fly from the wrath of the king, fly from the anger of Jehosheba, the wife of Elkanah, that was next to the king." That lady vexed me sore when days of peace allowed her pride free rein. But the crown has fallen from her head, her husband, Elkanah, lies slain upon the lofty fields. And now she is desolate in widowhood and can understand the pain of Miriam, my wife, who weeps for me, her loved one, in his roamings like a wandering bird. But whither shall I fly? Shall Jerusalem cry freedom upon me to enter her gates? Behold, Ahaz has cried freedom there to let his people sin, to serve new gods which he has chosen—Darmesek, god of Aram, to whom he has built an altar in Jerusalem, saying: "These are the gods of Aram's kings, who help them; to them shall I sacrifice, and they shall help me also." And in every corner of Jerusalem and in all the cities of Judah he has raised high places. And the people walk in darkness and rebellion, sacrificing and burning incense to Darmesek, god of Aram, and to Milcom, the abomination of the Ammonites, and to their Baals and Ashtoreths, the idols of the nations. He it is, King Ahaz, who makes Judah sin, and in all the places where he reigns the land rises against me. And shall I choose to dwell in Ephraim? There too snares are set to trap me. For the prophets of Beth-El and the company of priests stand everywhere on guard, and woe upon me if my name become known to my enemies, for they will not be sated with my flesh. My heart breaks within me for Judah, and of Ephraim it shall be said: "They kiss their calves and slaughter men." For the blood of man is worthless in their sight, but they love their calves, their priests, their prophets and their Baals, and they have become as slaves nailed to the doorposts of a house of evil, eternal slaves to idols. Behold, the year of

Jubilee has come to summon every man to return to his inheritance, yet Ephraim is joined to idols, still arrogant in foreign bonds, and refuses to return to the Lord, the inheritance of their fathers. Alas, there is no freedom for Judah, no Jubilee for Ephraim, and no redemption for my soul. Wherefore the Lord has cried freedom to the sword, to lay the land of Judah waste; and the trumpet resounds in the house of evil, the trumpet of the Jubilee, and Ephraim shall be carried unto Assyria.'

The lone figure ceased pouring out his heart to God, and his servant approached him trembling and impatient, saying: 'Think of some plan, Uzziel, my master, for danger is nigh. Behold, our mortal enemies surround us, encircling the hill below. And though I know our enemies will not attempt to climb this place, which even the wild beasts cannot reach, how can that save us? Here on this fastness we sit as though on scorpions, fearing to descend because of our pursuers who lie in ambush. You see now, Uzziel, my master, that my words have come to pass. For how many times, my master, have I said to you: "Whom have you here, what have you here that you perch like an eagle on this tooth of rock, eating your bread in desolation and drinking your water in fear? Hasten and find yourself another refuge." And you promised to tell me the name of your wife in Zion, and to send me there to reveal to her your hiding place, that she might give you counsel from afar. If you had only sent me when you promised, perhaps by now your wife might have found a place of refuge for you, if she remains as faithful to you as you to her. But words count nothing, if deeds will not bring salvation.'

'This is indeed no time for words,' Uzziel answered. 'Go to the crag's edge and lie upon the ground, and listen closely to what our pursuers say. Then tell me what you hear, for I know what must be done.'

The servant did his master's bidding and listened intently until the sound of voices rose to his ear. Then he returned to the lone man and said: 'I heard the confused noise of many men, but one voice I heard, saying: "We stand on guard in vain.

It would appear that the lion of Amana has left his lair, and made his way to the valley. Wherefore let us disperse and seek him among the thickets." Thus one spoke, but his fellow answered: "See, our master comes riding on his mule, and armed with sword and bow." '

Then Uzziel stood thinking for some moments, until rousing himself he said to his servant: 'Come, I will meet my enemies with cunning. Take the horn from my room, and blow a great blast, so that they who lie in ambush will say: The sound of the horn is to warn the hunter of his peril, that he may hurry away to safety. Meanwhile I shall arm myself with sword, bow and arrows ready for the fray, and descend upon my enemies and cry peace upon them, declaring myself innocent of harm. But if they believe me not and do battle with me, then shall I indeed be innocent before the Lord. And I shall hurl myself upon them, striking right and left, that those who pursue me without cause shall die with me. For what does it profit me to prolong my life?'

Obedient to his command, the servant took the horn and sounded a great blast, and then a second, and a third. And just as Uzziel had foreseen, so did it come to pass. For those in ambush scattered among the thickets, seeking the lion of Amana. And Uzziel waited till he could not bear it more, then ordering his servant to lower the ladder, he descended armed to the hilt like a man of war, prepared for evil or for good.

THE PLOT OF 'THE HYPOCRITE'

THE story opens in the poverty-stricken setting of a way-side inn. The owner, Jeroham, was formerly a rich merchant who entrusted his affairs during his long business trips to an upstart manager, Gaal. The latter, the rejected lover of Jeroham's daughter, Sarah, now Joseph's widow, in consequence contrived to ruin Jeroham, who was stripped of all his possessions. Joseph, however, had a faithful friend, Saul, who advanced him money to acquire the inn, and secured a post for Joseph in the service of the local Baron. Sarah bore three children, Naaman, Ruhamah and Raphael, the youngest of whom was betrothed at birth to Saul's daughter. But Gaal so poisoned the Baron's mind against Joseph that he was dismissed and died of a broken heart.

Saul keeps faith with his dead friend, and sends his son, Naaman, to study agriculture. Naaman is about to complete his studies, return to support his family and bring Gaal to justice, when the latter induces Naaman's friend, Zimon, to plant false documents in Naaman's room and denounce him as a spy. Naaman is arrested and disappears, while rumour reaches Jeroham that he has been drowned. Gaal uses the opportunity to spread slander against Jeroham, and ruin his trade in the inn. He plans to force the old man to surrender documents which could incriminate him, at the same time hoping to marry the widowed Sarah.

The burden of poverty compels Jeroham—via the agency of Nehemiah, a champion of enlightenment—to beg a former business colleague, Obadiah, to buy his inn. But the latter, too, is under Gaal's influence and returns only abuse. Gaal's villainy is supported and excelled by that of his son-in-law, Zadok, an arch-hypocrite. The latter, whose real name is Hophni, having already deserted two wives, has usurped the name and credentials of a famous Palestinian scholar and Rabbi who had died on a journey from the Holy Land. His base schemes are furthered by his servant Levi, who plans to marry Joseph's daughter Ruhamah, who, as Zadok learns from a letter ad-

עיט צבוע

מאתי

אברהם בן־יקותיאל מאפו

איש קאוונא

ווילנא

בדפוס ר' יוסף ראובן ב"ר מנחם מן ראם

שנת תרי"ז לפ"ק

АИТЪ-ЦАВУА

т. е.

Пестрая птица или Ханжа. Соч. Абрама Мапу.

ВИЛЬНО.

Въ Типографіи Р. М. Ромма.

1857.

Title-page of the first edition of *The Hypocrite*

By courtesy of the Bodleian Library, Oxford

dressed to Jeroham which he has intercepted, is due to receive a large inheritance from her relative Michael in London. Zadok, accordingly, advises Levi to plant some incriminating jewellery in Jeroham's house, and have him arrested for theft. Without her grandfather's guardianship Ruhamah will fall an easy prey to Levi. This jewellery, which formerly belonged to Sarah, had been taken by Obadiah in part payment of his debt. Obadiah had given it to his grand-daughter Elisheba, who, being deeply in love with Naaman, had wanted to return it to Ruhamah, his sister, but had been robbed of it while journeying home.

By the eve of Passover Jeroham's household is in such dire straits that even the necessities for the festival are wanting. Suddenly Naaman arrives, disguised as Zimon. He explains that he had, himself, spread the rumour of his death, the better to pursue his revenge on Gaal. He describes how he has rescued Eden, Obadiah's son, from a band of robbers, while he was conveying a large sum of money for the Baron. He has returned home with rich gifts from the Baron, as well as a present for Elisheba from her father Eden, and one for Eden's wife, Zibiah. He has also brought a letter from Eden to Obadiah, urging that Elisheba marry only a man of her own choosing, and warning Obadiah against Gaal. Saul arrives the same day to swell the happiness of Jeroham's family, and intimates that, as a widower, he is ready to marry Sarah.

Their joy is shattered, however, by the arrest of Jeroham and Sarah, charged with stealing the jewellery which Levi has concealed in his home. Obadiah finally takes pity on them and offers bail, but he is preceded by the Baron's wife. But Naaman, now known as Zimon, can make no progress in winning Obadiah's consent to his marrying Elisheba. The matter is complicated by Gaal's desire that she should wed his own son Zerah, while Zadok, whose wife has just died, is also angling for her. Moreover Elisheba is prejudiced against the supposed Zimon, being in love with Naaman. She is also suspicious of Zimon's relationship with Ruhamah.

Meanwhile Zaphnath, the proprietress of a neighbouring

inn, who is the principal agent behind the campaign of slander directed against Jeroham's family, is conducting an illicit affair with Levi. Her husband, Jerahmeel, is a pious but unpractical man who has been wandering through many lands for seven years, and has now returned in search of the wicked Hophni, alias Zadok, who is wanted for murder, theft, forgery and bigamy. At Zaphnath's instigation, Jerahmeel is arrested and thrown into prison. Levi contracts a fever, and before his death reveals something of Zadok's past. Simultaneously Zadok and Gaal become estranged, while Zaphnath, whose adultery is exposed, flees to London with Emil, a worthless rake who is anxious to conceal his Jewish origin. They are accompanied by Zerah, Gaal's son, who has fled the country after stealing some money deposited with Zadok for safekeeping.

On the ship bound for London they meet Naaman and Ruhamah, as well as Azriel, a young scholar returning from the Holy Land with Shiphrah, whom he had saved from drowning in the Sea of Galilee. They are on their way to collect an inheritance bequeathed to them by Michael. They are accompanied by Heman, a native of Italy, but who has lived in Turkey and Palestine, where he befriended Azriel. He is travelling with his sister in search of Alkum, alias Hophni, alias Zadok, who has deserted her. The party is completed by Shlomiel, who is also seeking Hophni. Suddenly a dreadful storm springs up, and Zaphnath and Emil are washed overboard, but not before Zerah has revealed their secret and Levi's disclosures about Zadok.

Even before they return from London, enough of Zadok's duplicity has leaked out to alienate even the stubborn and bigoted Gaddiel; while for his part Zadok reveals something of Gaal's wickedness. Yet Obadiah still pins his faith to Zadok's integrity and exerts pressure on Elisheba to marry him. Elisheba is very distressed, for she cannot return Naaman's affection as long as she believes him to be Zimon. Meanwhile Eden's death is reported, and Gaal makes overtures to his widow, Zibiah.

After many adventures the party from London returns with the inheritance, and Naaman reveals his real identity to Elisheba, informing her also that her father Eden is still alive. Even Obadiah is reconciled to their marriage, and on the wedding-day Eden, himself, appears. For the celebrations the Baron's castle is turned into a theatre to enact the play 'Joseph and his Brothers'. Zadok and Gaal are among the guests, the latter deliberately sitting next to Zibiah and urging her to forget the 'dead' Eden, and become his own wife. His proposal is meanwhile overheard by Eden. The Baron advances, and declares the time has come to put an end to strife. That the affair may be properly investigated he calls upon the contending parties, namely Gaal on the one hand, and on the other Obadiah and Jeroham, to submit their case to his judgement. Gaal comes forward and announces that as a gesture of reconciliation, he is willing to wed Zibiah, Eden's widow. At that moment Eden comes forth, takes off his disguise and denounces Gaal. Simultaneously Zadok's many accusers denounce him, so that even Obadiah's eyes are opened to his real nature. The final victory over the villains is complete, and their erstwhile victims handsomely avenged.

THE HYPOCRITE

THE guests were assembled around the table, seated each
according to his station. The old man was clad in a shroud-
like linen garment white as snow, whose upper edge—an
embroidered garland of beaten silver threads—encircled his
neck like a crown. His girdle was fastened with a silver brooch,
while his head was covered with a pure, white shawl, flecked
with sparkling silver, so that he sat upon his couch like a king
amid his courtiers. He first pronounced the benediction,
which the guests repeated; then raising the dish on high they
were reading in Aramaic the passage dealing with the bread of
affliction, when lo, a sound of lamentation was heard from the
room in which sat Zibiah with Elisheba. And the old man
trembled and sent Shemariah to see what was the matter. And
when Shemariah returned he related that the women were
weeping for Eden, for no news had arrived of what had
befallen him, and that was the cause of their distress.

'If that is so,' Zimon replied, 'I must read to them a letter
which I doubt if even Elisheba could make out alone, for Eden
himself wrote only a few lines at the end to testify that the
contents are true and dictated at his command.'

'Please go then,' the old man answered without enthusiasm,
'and read it to them to calm their spirits. But show me first
if it really is his hand.'

And Zimon took the letter from his pocket and showed it
to the old man, who said: 'This is indeed my son's writing in
the margin.'

So Zimon rose and went from the room carrying his stick.
And Zibiah and Elisheba said to him: 'You have already shown
us your kindness and good faith. Now give us words of comfort to calm our spirits, for we are much distressed.'

'Look, gentle Elisheba,' Zimon replied, 'I shall address myself
to you, not to your step-mother, for she is vexed with me.
The letter in my possession was dictated by your dear father,

but written by a soldier who, although of our people, had so little skill with a pen that the characters are scarcely recognizable. Why should you strain your lovely eyes on them? So I will read it to you and to the esteemed Zibiah, who may regard me with more favour in a little while. At the end of the letter there are a few lines written in Eden's hand to confirm all it contains. Now, good ladies, listen to the letter.'

'To Elisheba, my darling daughter, and to my beloved wife. May the Lord grant me life and peace, and protect me whether I dwell at home or travel abroad or walk in the valley of the shadow of death. May he carry me back safely to my father's house to bring joy to you all. That is my heart's desire and my prayer to God. There are times when a man forgets his Creator, dwelling in tranquillity and peace; but when danger threatens he repents, and remembers him constantly. Such has been my case, and now let me relate what has befallen me.

'Eight days ago the Baron entrusted me with a hundred thousand pieces of silver to pay the various officers who supply the troops with bread, meat and wine, and the horses with fodder. I set off on my way together with a servant lad to drive the horses. Towards evening the paths became slippery with rain and ice, and one of the horses caught his hoof on the treacherous path and was lamed, so that the carriage moved forward with difficulty. As the sun went down behind the mountains, we entered a vast forest, and very soon night descended upon us, plunging the path in darkness. As it was the first of the month there was no moon, while thick cloud blotted out the stars. Moreover, to my consternation, I perceived that we had wandered off the path and were lost in the pitch darkness. In my terror the curse of the holy Psalmist welled up in my heart: "Let their way be dark and slippery and the angel of the Lord pursuing them." And the cause of my fears was that the forest swarmed with desperate brigands, deserters from the army.'

'Alas! I feel dark terror stealing over me,' cried Elisheba. And Zibiah moaned: 'Alas! I am distraught!'

'Be calm and fear not,' Zimon replied. 'Hear me out, for all was well in the end.'

'Before we had continued much further our way led us among closely interwoven trees. When suddenly I heard the sound of whispering, and the noise of twigs breaking and footsteps in the undergrowth. Just then the boy who was driving the horses called out in a low, thin voice, which floated back to me: "May God on high protect us! The path has run out, and a gaping chasm yawns before us."

'The words of the lad terrified me. My stomach turned over as a wave of fear passed through me, and the dread of the Lord fell upon me. Had these three things combined against me, the blackness of the night, the treacherous path, and even spirits of evil pursuing us? But though my heart melted in fear, I encouraged the lad and said: "Have we not two pistols? If trouble comes we can defend ourselves, and the Lord will protect us with his shadow." Yet even as I spoke my teeth chattered and my hands shook, and the best plan seemed to remain where we were in absolute silence until the terror passed. But as though to terrify us more our horses whinnied. And suddenly I heard a voice crying: "Where are you leading us, you wretch? Can't you hear the horses neighing? Hurry, comrades, there's spoil here!"'

'My heart cries out for my father,' Elisheba exclaimed.

'My heart melts like wax within me,' Zibiah wailed.

And from the next room a voice could be heard reading: 'And we cried out to the Lord, the God of our fathers, and the Lord heard our cry, and perceived our sorrow, and our burden and our toil.'

'Do you hear, dear ladies?' said Zimon. 'The Lord listens to the voice of him that calls upon him from the depths. Thus did he listen to Eden's cry.'

Then he continued reading:

'As I heard those dreadful cries the fear of God took hold of me. The blood froze in my veins, my heart turned to stone. I put my finger on the trigger of my pistol, but my flesh crept with fear and my hands went limp. I determined to seek refuge in flight, but my legs seemed turned to lead. Therefore I entrusted my soul to my Creator, seeing that escape there was none, and death confronted me. Then before my eyes a terrible spectacle materialized—a wild man like an evil spirit or some offspring of death, his face covered with hair, a look of murder in his eyes, and every fibre of him tensed for slaughter. And in a hoarse voice he shouted to his comrades in evil: "Didn't I tell you we would find our quarry here?" Then he roared at me like a lion: "You there, all wrapped up in your shawl! Throw that armour off and bring out the money for us!" My strength ebbed away and my feet felt so weighed down with lead that I could not move. My eyes went black and my tongue clove to the roof of my mouth. I saw myself facing an untimely end, and as the murderer held my arm in a powerful grip I cried out: "Finish me off quickly then, and don't prolong the agony." But he merely shook me violently and handed me over to his four murderous companions, saying: "Let no one dare harm him. He may have hidden the money, or thrown it into some secret hiding place. So don't touch him till I search the carriage, even if I have to rip it to pieces."

'By then my soul was wearied of the murderers, and my body was damp with the fear of death. I broke out in a cold sweat, with the thought of murder numbing my spirit. My mind went blank and lost all power of cohesive thought. But from my heart's sorrow there welled up the memory of my old father, and your memory, my lovely daughter, and yours, too, my dear wife. I prayed to God for those beloved souls as long as I had strength. I wept from the depths of my heart and groaned in silence.'

At that point Elisheba and Zibiah could contain themselves no longer, and wept bitterly. But their lament was not heard in the other room above the reading of the guests. And Zimon said to Elisheba: 'Dry your pretty eyes, dear lady, for your lament need not continue long, and these tears will soon turn into boundless joy.'

Then he continued to read:

'But when my servant saw that the end was nigh, he

shouted aloud with all the strength of despair. Then one of the scoundrels said to the leader of the gang: "This bird is chirping. Give me leave to nip off his head, for why prolong his life? We will learn nothing of the money from him. Just say the word, master!" At that my servant summoned his remaining strength in one last desperate cry, and I did likewise. I cried for help, although I knew not whence my help would come. But hope springs eternal in the human breast.

'Nor was my hope in vain. For just as I prepared to surrender my life to these murderers, and entrust my soul to the God of all flesh, a rifle-shot rang out, followed by a lusty voice that cried: "Hurry up, men, with weapons at the ready! You heard that bitter cry for help, and our hands are against all accursed robbers. Hurry, and we'll take them alive!" And now a different tumult shattered the silence of the night. The robbers, five in number, returned the fire once or twice. But without time to reload their guns, their shots soon ceased. Their leader, however, hastily searched through my baggage, and snatching the bundle of notes equal in value to a hundred thousand pieces of silver fled for his life to some secret lair. Now the strange thing is that so long as death confronted me I withstood the darkness, yet as soon as I perceived that the mortal danger had passed, my spirit fainted and I know not what befell me. Therefore I can only repeat what my servant told me later. His account is as follows: When I saw that death had passed, I summoned all my strength and fled away, running and jumping like a stag. Then suddenly a fine young man rushed to the scene of slaughter like a fleet hind shouting: "This way, men!" I told him that five bandits had held my master up to ransom, and he girded his loins and pursued them headlong, his five friends at his heels. And he caught up with one of the robbers fleeing between the trees and smote the back of his neck with an iron-loaded stick. Nor was a second blow needed, for he dropped senseless in his tracks.'

Then Elisheba and Zibiah brightened and both looked at the handsome youth, and a smile appeared on Elisheba's lips as her gaze fastened on the stick and she saw through his disguise.

Even Zibiah was reconciled, while Elisheba rejoiced to feel her love increase a thousand times. But Zimon continued his reading:

'When I regained my senses I was lying quietly and safely in bed. Sitting at its head I saw a fine young man silently tending to my wants, as an attentive son would tend a beloved father. And when he saw me rouse myself, his eyes filled with tears of joy. But as soon as I perceived the light of day, I cried aloud as I remembered the hundred thousand pieces of silver which had fallen booty to the robber, without hope of return. And even the Baron, who had hastened to come to me and waited eagerly till I regained consciousness, shuddered as he heard of my loss. But the handsome youth, who had already shown his courage, now demonstrated his trustworthiness even more. For without a word he drew from his bosom the bundle of notes and laid them down before the Baron's eyes. In short, not a farthing was missing, and everyone was overjoyed. Even my servant did not know that the youth had recovered the robber's spoil, for he had done so secretly. Yet with this immense sum he could have become a great man in the land. His behaviour has been wonderful. Can I describe the honour which the Baron showed him? Words are superfluous, but the promise of the Baroness herself to be his patroness will give you some idea. And the name of this youth is Zimon. All this has been written at Eden's command.'

In the margin of the letter a few lines were added in Eden's hand:

'My dear ones, I write these lines as testimony that everything in this letter has been written at my dictation. The noble Zimon stands before you, therefore give him your blessing for his kindness and for saving my life. Zibiah, my dear wife, please accept from him the birthday gift which I have bought as a token of my undying love. And you, my dearest daughter, Elisheba, you have already met the good Zimon in the town of Amon at the theatre. And even there he told you of his readiness to make henceforth a pact of friendship with Jeroham, and espouse his cause. Therefore please accept these ornaments, which I send to you by his hand; and in return give your own jewellery to his friend Ruhamah, Sarah's daughter. And peace, prosperity and joy upon you, to Zibiah from your husband, and to Elisheba from your father, Eden.

Written from the army-camp of the Baron,

On this day of my salvation, the eighth day of Shevat, 1854.'

Elisheba was astounded at the coincidence, remembering that on the eighth day of Shevat she too had made a vow to return the jewellery to Ruhamah. And now she perceived that the same generous impulse had stirred her father's heart. But for the moment her mind was full of the wonderful deeds which her dear friend had done for her father. So she turned to Zibiah and said: 'What do you say now, mother, to all these marvels?'

'What can I say?' Zibiah answered delightedly. 'I can only repeat the remark our friend Zimon made to you. I would like to take them all in my arms, and embrace them. But how can we express our thanks to Zimon, who is responsible for this great salvation? Forgive me, dear youth, for my unkindness to you when first you entered my house. But now my feelings are quite changed, for the Lord sent you like an angel of salvation to my husband in his hour of need.'

'Indeed,' Elisheba answered, giving her hand to Zimon. 'It is not your stick, but my father's words that tell me that you are the angel that saved him.'

As she was speaking, the words of the readers from the next room could be heard recounting the mercies of the Lord in Egypt:

'If he had slain their first-born, without giving us their wealth, it would have been sufficient.'

And listening to the recitation Elisheba smiled charmingly and said: 'You too have shown us much wonderful kindness. You have saved my father's life, defeated the angel of death, recovered the stolen money and poured it out at the Baron's feet. You really have performed miracles, and I can in no way recompense you. We shall be ever in your debt.'

'You say you cannot recompense me?' Zimon repeated with a laugh. 'But you hold the key to my reward!'

And Elisheba understood his meaning and said: 'Please rejoin the guests, dear friend, and complete the reading with them. For we shall have the opportunity again to talk together.'

'I shall always respect your wishes,' replied Zimon, and with a winning smile he gave her his hand, then turned and left the room.

And Zibiah said to Elisheba: 'You see, my daughter, how completely my feelings have changed in a few moments, because of what this youth has done. I shall no longer scold you or rebuke you on his account, for he has done wonders for us.'

'He has indeed,' Elisheba answered. 'With his strong right arm he has preserved a beloved son for his father, a loving husband for his wife, and a merciful father for his daughter. And not only has he done all this, but to add joy to joy he has so changed your feelings towards me, that I know you will no longer vex me. Is not my father precious to us both? Then why should we be estranged without cause? Henceforth show me a mother's compassion, and I will show compassion in return.'

As she spoke Elisheba embraced Zibiah and kissed her, and continued: 'Do what I beg of you, and I shall call you mother.'

'For my part I welcome the reconciliation and I shall carry out your wishes,' Zibiah replied. 'And if you desire Zimon, as it appears you do, you have only to say the word and I shall try to win over your grandfather as soon as he has learned of Zimon's wonderful exploits. For the matter will depend on him, and Eden, his son, will not run counter to his wishes. So tell me what you desire.'

'What I desire!' Elisheba repeated thoughtfully. 'But leave me a while, mother, for my desires and thoughts are all confused. My mind is still so full that I cannot yet calm my spirit. So let us talk of it again at a better opportunity.'

Meanwhile Zimon had joined the guests in their reading,

and they completed the *Hallel* prayer and drank the second cup of wine according to custom. Then, having washed their hands, they ate the unleavened bread and bitter herbs, and partook of the rich and tasty fish which was set before them. Then Zimon read out the letter before all the assembled guests, and they were all astounded—even more so when they perceived the stout stick in his hand, with which he had cracked the robber-leader's head, and they kept glancing at him in wonder. The old man blessed him effusively, and all the guests sang his praises and lauded his deeds to the skies, that he had fought the robbers and prevailed. But the whole episode sorely distressed the old man, and his heart was full of dark foreboding that this Zimon might become an obstacle and stumbling-block to his plans. Meanwhile Reb Zadok sat silently as if in mourning, wearing an inscrutable expression. His face remained pale even though fire consumed his frame. Nor was his fear of Zimon groundless, for the latter was a thorn in his side, piercing him to the quick. Yet he kept silent, for what could he do? Should he praise Zimon's deeds? That would only hinder his own schemes. Should he belittle the praise? But then the guests would realize that he spoke from envy, and that while still in mourning for his dead wife, he had already fixed his eye on Elisheba. That evening too he must be on his guard, for the evening augured evil. Zimon he regarded as an angel of destruction who had come hither to wreck all the schemes which he had laid. But as he looked at the old man the latter's expression gave him hope. Zadok brightened and felt better, while a flicker of joy passed across his face, as though every fibre of his body were crying out: 'Elisheba shall yet be mine!'

Then Zimon said to the old man: 'I have still another message from your son, but it is addressed to you alone and no one else. His message was but short, and whenever you are ready, I will repeat his words in full.'

'Both a written and a verbal message,' replied the old man testily, looking at his watch. 'There is still time before we eat the last piece of unleavened bread. First trouble with a son, then with a daughter, and I have to worry about them all. But what can be done?'

With a sigh he rose from his couch and beckoned Zimon to follow him to his room, where Zimon gave him the letter, saying: 'This is not the time for me to speak, for I see you are in no mood for it; so read your son's letter.'

And Obadiah took the letter somewhat unwillingly and read as follows:

'My honoured and revered father! From the letter which I wrote to my wife and daughter you will realize what the noble youth Zimon has done for me. He is regarded as one of our younger men who are winning respect for Israel in high circles. But the actions of your trusted Gaal are quite the reverse. His poisonous tongue, which is like the bite of an adder, plotted to destroy me, and God alone be praised that I escaped his snares. You will not understand this secret now, but I shall hasten to enlighten you when the time comes. Then your eyes will be opened to the wicked Gaal's designs and you will take pity on Jeroham's house which Zimon, too, has taken under his wing. One more request I make of you, my honoured father. The time is drawing nigh for my beloved daughter Elisheba to marry; and I know that she is dear to you, and that you are anxious about her future. Be so good, therefore, as to decide nothing without consulting her wishes and mine. For as long as I am on the battle-front, my position is like that of a dangerously sick man, and my requests must be regarded as a testament. My life is in constant danger, but blessed be the Lord of my salvation, who will shelter me with his shadow, just as he sent the good angel, Zimon, to save me and my servant when death faced us. Soon we return to barracks, so expect no word from me until we leave again. After that your son, who is entirely devoted to you, looks forward eagerly to seeing you. Eden.'

'You have read it, sir, and you understand its meaning,' Zimon remarked, as the old man finished reading the letter.

'I understand it right enough,' the old man answered. 'The spirit of understanding comes with age. So leave me for a few moments, my friend, to commune with myself. In a little while I shall return, for it is time to pray to God, and that alone is true wisdom. We shall speak again about my son, who calls upon God for help in time of need, but forgets the great call which God makes to him. But leave me a little.'

And Zimon recognized the old man's confusion of mind, and left him to join the others at the festive table. There he found Elisheba, to whom Hogeh was just giving a letter and saying: 'Please read this letter written by my friend Azriel, with whom, I think, you are acquainted. This letter is both precious in itself and opportune, for it was composed on Mount Zion at the festival of Passover. So read it and see how great are his descriptive powers.'

So Elisheba took the missive from Hogeh and read as follows:

'In the year five thousand six hundred and thirteen according to the Jewish calendar, on the evening of the fourteenth day of the month of Aviv, the season of the ancient festival of Passover, I sit here on Mount Zion, a hill on the south side of Jerusalem, and make this solemn declaration with deep emotion. Peace upon you, mountains of Zion, Mount Moriah and the Mount of Olives, you sacred mountains that stand eternal as God's righteousness. Peace upon you, precious relics of antiquity, in whose name I made this journey, and whose remembrance fills my soul. Peace upon you, most precious of all dust, the dust of our fathers, whom I cherish.

'On the fourteenth day of the first month, the season of joy and gladness for our fathers in ancient times, the season of praise and thanksgiving to the Lord, who brought them forth from Egypt to settle upon this lovely land, the inheritance of their father Jacob—on this pleasant festival I sit upon Mount Zion, pencil in hand, to set down my inmost thoughts upon the page. And the mourning and desolate city of God looks down upon me from the north, through the veil of widowhood. Just as I had pictured her, so do I see her in all her holiness, as though mourning for her sacred desolation. My spirit aches to see her mounds forsaken, the forlornness of ancient times, and the desolation of each generation. Can this be Zion, so celebrated by the prophets who sprang from her? Enemies have destroyed her foundations, and fools have dispersed the words of her holy sons. But Mount Zion shall never crumble, nor shall the holy words be lost to Zion's sons. For these are the words of the living God, fixed in the heavens, lighting up the darkness like the stars. And even when heavy clouds conceal the stars, the spirit of wisdom shall shine forth, and pierce the blackness. The night shall vanish, and the light of God shine even as of old. Yea, a new light shall shine on Zion, which now lies desolate and mourning. The sons, which she bore in bewilderment, shall flock to her sacred ruins. They shall come streaming in from all the lands of the dispersion, for they are all her children, who bear her name upon their lips with every outpouring of prayer. They shall come to her and say that through all their sorrows and afflictions they have remembered her, and the love of Zion shall never be erased from their hearts. It is the love that springs from the delightful hope that hovers over her ruins, and whispers in our ears the consolation of Isaiah: "For the Lord shall comfort Zion: he will comfort all her waste places; and he will make her wilderness like Eden, and her desert like the garden of the Lord; joy and gladness shall be found therein, thanksgiving and the voice of melody."

'But the word of the Lord has not yet come, and so I stand on the appointed mountain and meditate on ancient times when the Passover was prepared for those that came to celebrate it, and I among them in imagination. And the magic of my dream conjures up a vision of great crowds thronging the streets and market-places of Jerusalem. The shadows lengthen, the day ebbs away and the sun, that faithful witness in heaven, announces that the time has come to serve the Lord. And a voice cries out in the gates: "Hurry, you people of the God of Abraham, and all who fear the word of the Lord both near and far, hurry to celebrate the Passover at the appointed season." And at the sound vast crowds emerge from the city of God, the princes of Judah from their marble palaces, and the poor of the land from their tents. At such a time both rich and poor are equal, for the spirit of the Lord gathers them all. Together they bring their paschal lamb to their families and their fathers' houses, and together they stream into the courtyards of the Lord to the sound of drums, viols and cymbals. Come, you that celebrate, and let us ascend the mountain to God's temple, to give thanks to him that is sanctified in glory, who singled us out to be his people. How delightful is this mighty voice of Israel, chanting the hymn of praise in the holy temple! And in the city's streets I hear the sound of voices crying: "Eat, friends, of the Passover, with all your hearts. Eat of the roasted meat with the unleavened bread and bitter herbs, but break not the bone thereof." And I, who had eaten nothing since morning, devoured the holy flesh with relish. The poor ate thereof and were sated; and my soul, too, was sated with joy, to mingle with this holy congregation, and to sing the stirring songs of valour amidst young and old.

'This is the heavenly vision which my imagination conjured up concerning Mount Zion and her assemblies. All the delights of ancient times welled up and lived before my eyes. Hurrah! I thought—wake up, my soul, and awaken the love of the eternal people. Remember the days of old, that they may bring comfort at the present time. And you too, O sacred Hebrew tongue, don your holy garb and your spirit of noble grace, and sing to your lover, the youth of Israel, borne on the arms of God since the days of Egypt. Make your voice resound, that your words be heard to the very ends of the earth, wherever the sound shall reach. But sing your song only for him that loves you, for the people that has chosen you, for they are all your delight. Hurrah! my spirit marches proudly, walking the eternal paths of old. And with the power of imagination I hear a rustling from the grave, a cry from out the rock, the voice of the world's dead that sleep in the dust of the ground, rising rejuvenated from the ashes of death, and living before me in my sight. This is the great cry, which breaks forth from the Hebrew tongue to her people, resounding as in the days of her youth.

'I plan to remain in Zion throughout the month of Aviv. Then I shall travel the road of God to the Jordan and Hermon, to celebrate the Feast of Weeks in Tiberias. And when the festival has passed I shall make my way to Damascus, God willing. For the heart of man may plan his course, but God alone directs his steps to wheresoever he wishes.

'May God be with me in all my paths, that my way be smooth. And you, dear friend of my youth, accept my best wishes, and my blessing be upon you and upon our friend, the learned doctor Hogeh, wherever he may be. I shall remember you from the land of Jordan, so think kindly of me, for I am your devoted friend, Azriel.'

After finishing the letter, Elisheba handed it back to Hogeh and gracefully added: 'Would that letters such as this might appear more often in our literature! For only such refinement of language will teach the youth of Israel good taste and fine understanding, and inspire their minds. But not so the harsh style which ruins the taste of the learned, and robs the language of its beauty. Azriel writes in an exalted style, and the words of his letter might well be counted among the holy things of Israel.'

'The holy things of Israel?' replied Shubal indignantly. 'It is not for women to declare what is good or what is holy. Such judgements can be given only by the pious men of the community, and they pour out their wrath against these refined and polished writings, condemning both the literary gems and their noisy authors equally to perdition. Yet you, Elisheba, declare that they may be counted among the holy things of Israel. Who then is destroying holiness with worthless phrases?'

'What is all this quarrelling?' the old man asked.

'It is no quarrel,' Shubal replied. 'But a slip of the tongue. Your daughter erred in thinking that fine language might be counted among the holy things of Israel, while I condemned all such authors and everything to do with them out of hand.'

'Why do you persecute them so relentlessly?' replied Jair. 'Once you defended them. Have you changed so much that you can cruelly assign them all to hell? Do you not hear their bitter cries?'

'Even from the depths of hell they would still cry out in

elegant phrases!' Shubal retorted caustically. 'Nor will they be there alone, for those who honour them will accompany them down. But why should I joke about things which are so serious? In my youth I toyed with their glowing coals, and so scorched my fingers that even today I feel the scars. All who look for righteousness in them are deluded; for their fine words are like deadly flies that hover boldly about the flowers of paradise, daring even to penetrate the sanctuary and pollute the fragrant oil. They are saturated with lies, they shoot out their lips against both God and man, and tear out holy ideas root and branch, leaving not a shred, and rejecting them utterly. But what I always say to these slanderers is this: Do not malign in secret, but bring forth your arguments, and show them squarely to our brethren who remain faithful to Israel. Put them before us naked, without shrouding their faces in a mantle of righteousness, as Azriel has done in this letter. Then they can see their nakedness and be ashamed. For even Azriel covers himself with fig-leaves which he has sewn together in this letter, and the secrets of ancient days he has moulded into a healing salve to hide the truth.'

'You are a bigot, my dear Shubal,' answered Jair, 'and you wrap yourself in zeal for God like a cloak. But your zeal for God is really zeal against your fellow men. What harm do you find in Azriel that you deride him and despise his fine words?'

'Listen to me, Jair, my friend though my opponent,' Shubal answered, 'you know that I, too, once trumpeted the praise of fine words and elegant language. But once my eyes were opened by experience to see the world clearly, I so learned to disdain them, and despise their honeyed sweetness, that they became anathema to me. For they are destroying Israel. And as for Azriel, Hogeh's friend, I am angry with him because he is a youth to whom God has given understanding and material advantages. I told him time and again: "Stay here and hold fast to your faith." But he was foolish and wandered off abroad. Now he is in the Holy Land, with the result that he transmits his visions from Mount Zion to Othniel, his friend, and sets him a fine example! But what is the good of making speeches? Take away the roses, I say, before the thorns begin to prick our young!'

'You are one of us indeed,' replied the old man. 'Would that there were more zealots like you in Israel. All these fancy phrases are woman's wisdom, and quite suitable for my daughter Elisheba; but the Lord did not intend it for men. If only Azriel had sent us some new legal decision, then I might have praised him.'

'Would you have Azriel send us some new decision from across the sea?' asked Hogeh. 'Do we lack them here? Does not Zadok give us them by the hundred and Gaddiel by the thousand, so that they spring up all over the town like grass? But if the Lord has not granted such a faculty to Azriel, let him at least keep what he has; for he has been blessed with a princely share of refinement and understanding.'

'My dear doctor Hogeh,' the old man answered disapprovingly, 'I had not thought to hear such sentiments from you. But let us discuss the matter no longer, for sinful talk only leads to mischief.'

'And the tongue that speaks it will be rewarded with coals of fire,' Shubal added. 'I am distressed for you, Hogeh, especially as you are so excellent a physician.'

'Then you should heap coals of fire on your own lips,' Jair answered with a smile, 'for fire drives out fire! Or roll in the snow to cool the jealous ardour that burns in you. But in any case this is not the time for conversation.'

'Just so,' Zadok added. 'This is not the time to argue, but to complete the Passover.'

And as the old man supported him, they broke off the discussion until the Passover had been completed in every detail. Then they arose, and Naaman, still in the guise of Zimon, betook himself to the room to which Zibiah and Elisheba had retired, and addressed Elisheba in French: 'You know, dear lady, what I have done for your father, and that he could find no way of rewarding me. But your love is all the reward I want. So tell me whether I have the right to hope.'

Elisheba was confused, but also answered him in French: 'This is neither the place nor the time to speak about such matters. Meet me tomorrow at the home of the Baroness, and then I shall give you a proper answer.'

'Hurrah,' answered Zimon still in French. 'I have listened most attentively, for to know your mind is what matters most for me now. I do hope that you will tell me plainly then that all my efforts have not been in vain.'

'Tomorrow and not now,' Elisheba repeated. 'And now you must retire.'

Just then the old man, who regarded Zimon as a thorn in his side, entered the room and said: 'Night was created for sleep or study only—as the sages say. All other talking is unnecessary.'

'Quite right, sir,' Zimon replied. 'But I was talking of your son, and so my words bring his daughter fresh life. Is that sinful?'

The old man laughed and quoted the psalmist: ' "Show forth thy loving-kindness in the morning and thy faithfulness every night." But now, my young friend, I have given orders that your couch be prepared in the loft. So take yourself up there now and retire to sleep.'

With that the old man called to his servant Shemariah and bade him conduct Zimon to the place which had been prepared for him in the loft. So Shemariah put a candle in a silver candlestick to light the way for Naaman, took him up to the room prepared for him and arranged his couch, but sighing all the time. And when Naaman asked him why he sighed, he answered not a word, but taking the candle in his hand he tiptoed to the door, and opened it suddenly to find Zipporah!

'What do you want, Zipporah?' Shemariah asked her.

'Oh, nothing!' the girl answered. 'Only that I slept here yesterday with my mistress Elisheba, and left a white handkerchief here.'

'Then why are you so anxious about it?' Shemariah continued. 'Surely you can find it tomorrow.'

'I hope so,' Zipporah replied, and went downstairs.

After she had gone Shemariah said to Zimon: 'You see,

yourself, that you are regarded as a pest in this house, and that Zadok alone commands respect here. I'm sure Zipporah was sent to listen behind the door to what I say to you. So I had better not linger here or Zibiah will box my ears again, as she has already done once today because I was praising you in the presence of Elisheba, who is always glad to listen to me. So consider your plans well, sir, and do what must be done for your own good and for her good too—for you need Elisheba. If God answers my request, I shall be more than ready to become your servant this time next year.'

'How good of you!' Naaman replied, putting his hand on the servant's shoulder. 'Then say a prayer for us. Perhaps the Lord will listen to your plan and bring it to pass.'

'Would that he may,' Shemariah sighed. 'This very day I promised Meir the Wonder-Worker eighteen pence if he would intercede to bring it about. So we'll see just how power-ful he is. And if he deceives me this time, I shall tell everybody that it is useless to bring him gifts. And many people will listen to me, so that his losses will be great.'

Naaman could scarcely suppress a smile at the servant's credulity, but he said: 'Don't worry about Meir the Wonder-Worker, for I'm sure your gift will not be in vain. It will cer-tainly bring me what you asked from him. Then many people will hear of the miracle which he has performed and hasten to bring him gifts, so that faith in him will grow daily.'

He had scarcely finished when Zibiah's maid came to sum-mon Shemariah, saying: 'You know how grumpy the old man is. You had better hurry down to him.'

'Yes, hurry down to him,' Naaman added in his turn.

And Shemariah answered angrily: 'There's no peace and quiet for an old man.' And turning away, he went downstairs.

BIBLIOGRAPHY

E. AUERBACH, *Mimesis*, English version, New York, 1953.

R. BRAININ, *Abraham Mapu*, Piotrokow, 1900.

R. A. BRAUDES, *Ha-Dat we-ha-Ḥayyim*, Lemberg, 1885. (First published 1876-7.)

M. E. CHASE, *Life and Language in the Old Testament*, London, 1956.

I. COHEN, *History of the Jews in Vilna*, Philadelphia, 1913.

D. DAVIDSON, *The Social Background of the Old Testament*, Hebrew Union College Press, 1942.

I. DAVIDSON, *Parody in Jewish Literature*, New York, 1907.

M. DOLITSKY, *Shebeṭ Sofer*, Vienna, 1883.

S. R. DRIVER, *An Introduction to the Literature of the Old Testament*, 9th ed., Edinburgh, 1920.

S. M. DUBNOW, *History of the Jews in Russia and Poland*, Philadelphia, Vol. I, 1916; Vol. II, 1918.

O. EISSFELDT, *Einleitung in das Alte Testament*, Tübingen, 1934.

I. ERTER, *Ha-Zofeh le-Beit-Yisrael*, Vienna, 1858.

J. FICHMAN, *Anshei Besorah*, Tel-Aviv, 1938.
Allufei ha-Haskalah, Tel-Aviv, 1952.

E. M. FORSTER, *Aspects of the Novel*, London, 1927.

H. T. FOWLER, *A History of the Literature of Ancient Israel*, New York, 1912.

J. FRANK, 'Le-Toledotaw Shel Mapu', in *Ha-Shiloah*, XXXIV, 1918.

A. FRIEDBERG, in *Sefer ha-Zikronot*, Warsaw, 1899.

S. GINSBURG, *The Life and Works of Moses Hayyim Luzzatto*, Philadelphia, 1931.

S. D. GOITEIN, *Omanut ha-Sippur ba-Miḳra*, Jerusalem, 1956.

J. L. GORDON, *Kol Shirei J. L. Gordon*, Tel-Aviv, 1929.

C. H. GRABO, *The Technique of the Novel*, Scribner's, U.S.A., 1928.

H. GRAETZ, *Geschichte der Juden*, Leipzig, Vol. V, 1895; Vol. XI, 1900. English revised edition, *History of the Jews*, London, 1891–2.

G. B. GRAY, *The Forms of Hebrew Poetry*, London, 1915.

L. GREENBERG, *The Jews in Russia*, Vol. I, New Haven, 1944.

S. HALKIN, *Modern Hebrew Literature*, New York, 1950.

J. G. VON HERDER, *Vom Geist der Ebräischen Poesie*, 2 vols., Dessau, 1782–3.

H. JAMES, *The Art of Fiction*, New York, 1948.

A. KAPLAN, *Ḥayyei Abraham Mapu*, Vienna, 1870.

J. KLAUSNER, *Yoẓerim u-Bonim*, Vol. I, Tel-Aviv, 1925. *Historiah Shel ha-Sifrut ha-'Ibrit ha-Ḥadashah*, Vol. III, 2nd revised ed., Jerusalem, 1953.

J. A. KLAUSNER, *Ha-Novelah ba-Sifrut ha-'Ibrit*, Tel-Aviv, 1947.

M. KLEINMAN, 'Abraham Mapu we-Hashpa'ato', in *Demuyot we-Ḳomot*, 2nd ed., London, 1928.

E. KÖNIG, 'Style of Scripture', in Hastings, *Dictionary of the Bible*, extra vol., 1904, pp. 156–69.

P. LAḤOWER, *Meḥkarim we-Nisyonot*, Warsaw, 1925. *Toledot ha-Sifrut ha-'Ibrit ha-Ḥadashah*, 6th ed., Tel-Aviv, 1946.

F. R. LEAVIS, *The Great Tradition*, London, 1948.

J. LEPIN, in *Ḳeset ha-Sofer*, Berlin, 1857.

S. LEVIN, *Childhood in Exile*, London, 1929.

R. LIDDELL, *A Treatise on the Novel*, London, 1949.

M. L. LILIENBLUM, ' 'Olam ha-Tohu', in *Ha-Shaḥar*, IV, 1874.

A. LODS, *The Prophets and the Rise of Judaism*, New York, 1937.

M. H. LUZZATTO, *Migdal 'Oz*, Leipzig, 1837. *La-Yesharim Tehillah*, Amsterdam, 1743.

D. B. MACDONALD, *The Hebrew Literary Genius*, Princeton, 1933.

S. MAIMON, *The Autobiography of Solomon Maimon*, English ed., London, 1954.

A. MAPU, *Kol Kitebei Abraham Mapu*, Tel-Aviv, 1950.

I. G. MATTHEWS, *Old Testament Life and Literature*, New York, 1934.

J. MEISL, *Haskalah*, Berlin, 1919.

G. F. MOORE, *The Literature of the Old Testament* (Home University Library), London and New York, 1913.

E. MUIR, *The Structure of the Novel*, London, 1949.

W. O. E. OESTERLEY and T. H. ROBINSON, *An Introduction to the Books of the Old Testament*, London, 1934.

J. PALMER, *Ben Jonson*, London, 1934.

D. PATTERSON, 'The Use of Songs in the Novels of Abraham Mapu', in the *Journal of Semitic Studies*, Vol. I, No. 4, October, 1956.

'Moses Mendelssohn's Concept of Tolerance', in *Between East and West*, London, 1958.

'Israel Weisbrem: A Forgotten Hebrew Novelist of the Nineteenth Century', in the *Journal of Semitic Studies*, Vol. IV, No. 1, January, 1959.

'Some Religious Attitudes Reflected in the Hebrew Novels of the Period of Enlightenment', in the *Bulletin of the John Rylands Library*, Vol. 42, No. 2, March, 1960.

'The Portrait of Hasidism in the Nineteenth-Century Hebrew Novel', in the *Journal of Semitic Studies*, Vol. V, No. 4, October, 1960.

'Hebrew Drama', in the *Bulletin of the John Rylands Library*, Vol. 43, No. 1, September, 1960.

The Foundations of Modern Hebrew Literature, London, 1961.

'Some Linguistic Aspects of the Nineteenth-Century Hebrew Novel', in the *Journal of Semitic Studies*, Vol. VII, No. 2, Autumn, 1962.

'The Portrait of the "Saddik" in the Nineteenth-Century Hebrew Novel', in the *Journal of Semitic Studies*, Vol. VIII, No. 2, Autumn, 1963.

The Hebrew Novel in Czarist Russia, Edinburgh University Press, 1964.

'Epistolary Elements in the Novels of Abraham Mapu', in *The Annual of Leeds University Oriental Society*, Vol. IV, 1964.

J. PERL, *Megalleh Ṭemirin*, Vienna, 1819, and *Boḥan Ẓaddik*, Prague, 1838.

R. H. PFEIFFER, *Introduction to the Old Testament*, New York, 1948.

C. RABIN, ' 'Olelot le-Toledot ha-Dramah ba-Haskalah ha-Germanit', in *Melilah*, Vol. V, 1955.

'Ibrit Medubberet Lifenei 125 Shanah, in the series *Leshonenu la-'Am*, Jerusalem, 1963.

J. S. RAISIN, *The Haskalah Movement in Russia*, Philadelphia, 1913.

A. RUPPIN, *The Jews in the Modern World*, London, 1934.

S. SACHS, 'Toledot Abraham Mapu', in supplement to the 30th year of *Ha-Ẓefirah*, Warsaw, 1903.

G. G. SCHOLEM, *Major Trends in Jewish Mysticism*, Jerusalem, 1941.

Shabbetai Ẓebi, Tel-Aviv, 1957.

A. SHA'ANAN, *'Iyyunim be-Sifrut ha-Haskalah*, Merhavia, 1952.

N. SLOUSCHZ, 'Miktab Mapu le-Aḥiw', in *Ha-Zeman*, 1908.

The Renascence of Hebrew Literature (translated from the French), Philadelphia, 1909.

P. SMOLENSKIN, *Ha-To'eh be-Darekei ha-Ḥayyim*, Warsaw, 1905. (First published 1868–70.)

S. SPIEGEL, *Hebrew Reborn*, New York, 1930.

R. ST. JOHN, *Tongue of the Prophets*, New York, 1952.

S. STREIT, *Ba-'Alot ha-Shaḥar*, Tel-Aviv, 1927.

A. S. WALDSTEIN, *The Evolution of Modern Hebrew Literature*, New York, 1916.

M. WAXMAN, *A History of Jewish Literature*, New York, Vol. I, 2nd ed., 1938; Vol. II, 2nd ed., 1943; Vol. III, 2nd ed., 1945.

S. WERSES, ' 'Iyyunim ba-Mibneh shel Megalleh Ṭemirin Ẓaddik' in *Tarbiẓ*, vol. 31, No. 4, 1962.

N. H. WESSELY, *Shirei Tif'eret*, Prague, 1829, and *Diberei Shalom we-Emet*, 1782–4.

A. YA'ARI, 'Abraham Mapu Bein Yehudei Arezot ha-Mizrah', in *Mo'zenayim*, III, 1931/2, part 48.

I. ZINBERG, *Toledot Sifrut Yisra'el*, Vol. 6, Tel-Aviv, 1960.

S. L. ZITRON, *Mapu u-Smolenskin we-Sippureihem*, Krakow, 1889.

　　Yozerei ha-Sifrut ha-'Ibrit ha-Hadashah, Vilna, 1922.

For bibliographical information on Mapu's letters see J. Klausner, *Historiah shel ha-Sifrut ha-'Ibrit ha-Hadashah*, in the bibliography to his article on Mapu.

INDEX

INDEX

The index covers the study of Mapu's life and work comprising Part One of this volume, but not the plot summaries and translations comprising Part Two. The names of Mapu's fictional characters, which are almost all drawn from the Bible, are printed in small capitals to distinguish them from Bible personages proper.

Abraham, 66

ACHAN, 65

ADAH, 33, 60

Adam ha-Cohen, 18

Ahabat Ziyyon, 3, *see also The Love of Zion*

Ahaz, 4, 41, 45, 49, 59, 65

AHIRA, 54

AHITUB, 54 f., 62, 89

Alexander II, 8, 9 n. 12, 22

Al-Hariri, 54

Al-Harizi, 54

AMMIHUD, 30

AMNON, 22, 29, 33 f., 41, 45 ff., 56 f., 71 ff., 82 f., 89, 91, 99 f.

Amon Pedagog, 19 n. 26, 24

Amos, Book of, 47 n. 39, 68 n. 13, 72 and n. 22

ASAPH, 55

ASENATH, 61

Ashmat Shomeron, 3, *see also The Guilt of Samaria*

Aufklärung, 5

'Ayit Zabu'a, 3, *see also The Hypocrite*

AZRIEL, 37, 87

AZRIKAM, 29, 54, 69, 71 f., 99

Bible, 6, 16, 19, 22 f., 26, 37 ff., 52, 58, 63 ff., 80, 85, 92, 96, 98, 105

Bing, I. B., 101

Bohan Zaddik, 54

Brandstätter, M. D., 106

Braudes, R. A., 106

BUKKIAH, 37, 60, 83, 92

Canticles, see Song of Songs

Cantonists, 8

CARMI, 38, 45, 54, 60, 83, 101

Chronicles, Book of, 39, 50 n. 50

DANIEL, 30, 61, 70

Diberei-Shalom we-Emet, 98

Dumas, Alexandre, the elder, 59, 102 f.

EDEN, 30, 32

Edom, 50

ELIADA, 30, 34 f., 60, *see also* UZZIEL

Eliezer, Rabbi, 15

Elijah, Gaon of Vilna, 10 n. 14

ELIPHELET, 33 f., 57, 74

ELISHEBA, 31 f., 57, 61, 95

EMIL, 33, 95, 99

Enlightenment, 5, 7 ff., 17, 20, 27, 71 n. 19, 98, *see also Haskalah, Maskil(im)*

Ephrati, Joseph, 101

Erter, Isaac, 11, 54 f., 101 f.

Exodus, Book of, 46 n. 11, 66 n. 7, 98

Ezekiel, Book of, 69 n. 16

EZRA, 62, 103 n. 44